Cantor, Norman F.
  Inventing Norman Cantor: Confessions of a Medievalist

ACMRS Occasional Series, Volume 1
978-0-86698-293-1

Catalog: $28.95, £24
(discount 20%) $23, £19
Display copy (discount 50%) $14.47, £12

Name Bruce Forrest
(must pay before

For a full list of titles visit us online at:
acmrs.org/catalog

INVENTING NORMAN CANTOR:
CONFESSIONS OF A MEDIEVALIST

Arizona Center for Medieval and Renaissance Studies Occasional Publications

Volume I

INVENTING NORMAN CANTOR:
CONFESSIONS OF A MEDIEVALIST

by

NORMAN F. CANTOR

Arizona Center for Medieval and Renaissance Studies
Tempe, Arizona
2002

Library of Congress Cataloging-in-Publication Data
Cantor, Norman F.
   Inventing Norman Cantor: Confessions of a Medievalist / by Norman F.
   Cantor.
       p. cm.
   Includes index.
   ISBN: 0-86698-293-0 (alk. paper)
     1. Cantor, Norman F. 2. Historians—United States—Biography. 3.
   Middle Ages—Historiography—History—20th century. I. Title.

   D116.7.C36 A3 2002
   940.1'092–dc21
   [B]
                                                              2002027723

This book is made to last.
It is set in Garamond typeface, smythe-sewn, and printed
on acid-free paper to library specifications.

Printed in the United States of America

To the memory of my Princeton teacher
THEODOR E. MOMMSEN (d. 1958)
Humanist, Anti-Nazi, Philo-Semite

❖ CONTENTS ❖

PREFACE

This book has two main purposes. First of all, it aims to relate my life in medieval studies as student, teacher, scholar, and writer. This book is a sequel to my 1991 book, *Inventing the Middle Ages*, now in its fifteenth printing. That book told the story of medieval studies and its leaders from 1895 to 1965. This book covers the years 1948 to 2001 as filtered through the prism of my memory.

The second main purpose of this book is to communicate my experience as a provost or dean in major research universities and to describe the inner workings of campus administration.

Drawing upon my personal experiences, my inquiries, and my perceptions as a historian, I have tried in this book to examine the American university and academic culture and the changes the campuses have undergone since the 1940s.

I wish to thank the following for their critical readings of earlier drafts: William Bowsky, Charles Dellheim, Ed Doctorow, Maurice Eash, Gail Eisenberg, Ron Hirsch, Brian Patrick McGuire, Judith Potter, Nancy Silver Shalit, Arthur Williamson, Lynda Zweben-Howland.

Robert Hanning and Kate Ludwig-Jansen gave me some interesting perspectives on the recent generational development of medieval studies.

Dee Ranieri typed the manuscript and prepared the electronic version for the publisher.

BIOGRAPHICAL NOTE

Norman F. Cantor was born in Winnipeg, Manitoba, Canada, in 1929, the only child of a cattle rancher. After graduating first in his class in Honors Arts from the University of Manitoba in 1951, he entered the doctoral program in medieval history at Princeton and was chosen best student in the Princeton Graduate School in 1953. After studying at Oxford and doing research in London on a Rhodes Scholarship, he returned to Princeton to teach in 1955-60 and received his Ph.D. there in 1957. In 1960 at the age of thirty, Cantor became the youngest person to get tenure in the Columbia University History Department. Later on he entered university administration and served as a provost or dean in three major universities. He concluded his academic career by teaching medieval studies, legal history, comparative literature, and sociology at New York University for twenty-two years and retired from teaching in December 1999. Cantor took up residence in South Florida and entered a third career as a professional writer of history books about the Middle Ages. By 2001 he had become the most widely read academic medieval historian in the English language.

Among his honors were being appointed as Fulbright Professor at Tel Aviv University in 1987, having one of his books cited for "literary excellence" by the National Book Critics Circle, and being chosen one of the dozen best teachers in the New York University College of Arts and Science in 1991.

Norman Cantor has published eighteen books, ten of which are about the Middle Ages. *In the Wake of the Plague*, hailed by the Journal of the American Medical Association as "fascinating," was a *New York Times* best-seller.

Cantor's wife Mindy is an art historian; his son Howard is a farmer in northern Vermont, and his daughter Judy is a bilingual (Spanish) jounalist in Miami. He has a grandson Max, Howard Cantor's son.

❖ 1 ❖

THE LAST
ROUNDUP

O n the Wednesday before Labor Day 1951, I sat in the saddle
again unwillingly although I knew that in just a few long,
dung-filled days, my life would be forever transmuted. I was battling
mosquitoes and inhaling air, thick with the smell of manure and dust,
from an hour before dawn to the falling dusk that came at 9:00 P.M. in
the northern clime of the Interlake District of central Manitoba. On the
shores of Lake Manitoba 100 miles north of the U.S. border, I was
pressed once again to act the role of miserable and incompetent cowboy
on my father's small ranch in the Metis (French-Indian "half breed")
village of St. Laurent.

There my father, product of a *shtetl* near Minsk in Belarus, had each
summer since 1939 raised three hundred purebred Hereford "white
face" beef cattle, fattening them on the long grass and the pure water
from an artesian well on his land. At the end of the summer he shipped
his beasts to the big cattle market in St. Boniface, Manitoba, the third
largest in Anglophone America after the Chicago Stockyards and the
new beef center emerging in Omaha, Nebraska.

During the War, buyers of beef for the American army had come north five hundred miles from Minneapolis over the old Great Northern Railroad, whose tracks were laid in 1870, and had driven prices sky high by buying everything in sight that was on the hoof. The good days were now over, had been since 1946, after the freewheeling Americans left. Now the four big packing plants in St. Boniface had formed a monopoly to drive prices down in a nakedly capitalist country that knew no antitrust laws.

It was a struggle for my father and the other small ranchers in the Interlake Country in the 1950s. Beef prices were depressed; a few cents per pound fluctuation could make or break them. So they held onto their animal cargo until Labor Day weekend, over the summer fattening as much as possible on the long grass the beautiful Herefords and the sleek Black Angus, the other prime meat carcass, before shipping their precious beasts to market with a wing and a prayer, as they sang during the War.

My father, his Metis ranch hand, and I mounted up in the darkness and with the critical help of a mongrel, mostly collie cattle dog, began driving my father's three hundred head of cattle through the front gate of the ranch onto the cattle drive lane beside the gravel-surfaced, dusty public highway toward the railhead in St. Laurent nine miles away. We wanted to get the animals in the holding pens at the railhead by dusk, water them, feed them on rich oats to compensate for weight loss imposed by the cattle drive, and calm them down.

Then the steam-driven Canadian Pacific freight train would come through at 4:00 A.M. the next morning, and we would herd the cattle into the long cars bedded with thick soft hay and send them on to the 11:00 A.M. auction in the St. Boniface stockyards. There the leading brokerage firm was Slotin, Feinstein, and Spivak, the improbable Jews who represented my father and other small ranchers to the oligopolistic buying meatpackers.

Slotin's son was a genius physicist who worked on the atom bomb in Oak Ridge, Tennessee, and died there in 1947 of radiation from a nuclear laboratory explosion. A descendant of Feinstein married in Calfornia a Gentile woman named Dianne, who later became a big politico and by this marriage was able to pretend to the San Francisco and Los Angeles Jews that she was one of them. The Spivaks were a clan of local capitalists big in the postwar real estate boom in Winnipeg. One of them became an important politician and lawyer and was married to a beautiful and vivacious woman, who still sits in the Canadian Federal Senate.

Compared to these illustrious people my father was middle-class and humble. He endured in business because of the credit line the brokerage firm of Slotin and Company extended to him over the very long and horrible Canadian winter.

As the worst of three riders, I had the job of outrider, the one to chase down a wild range cow or steer when it got off the narrow path to the railroad terminal beside the dust-choked highway and headed into the bush. I had never learned to ride a horse properly. My father never sent me to riding school just as he never paid for auto driving school—I didn't learn to drive a car until I was twenty-six, which meant almost no dates.

As I followed the delinquent animal into the bush on precarious horseback, I was always afraid of falling off the horse or being slapped by the branch of an oak tree. Clouds of mosquitoes and black flies descended on me as I pursued, heart pounding, the range steer or cow into the bush. Without the cattle dog to take over, I would have accomplished nothing. I was there to "learn how to work," as my anxious mother called my miserable endeavors, more than really to help my father and his Metis "breed."

If fifteen minutes went by and I did not emerge from the bush behind the stray animal, my father would lose patience and go into the bush after the three of us, wayward steer or cow, barking cattle dog, and inept me. If things got desperate and the animal wasn't too big and strong, my father would lasso it, just like in the Hollywood movies. He was a superb and fearless cowboy and a marvelous rider. The year before he had gotten cocky and lassoed a big steer who dragged him off to the bush along the ground for a hundred yards while I looked on dumbstruck and characteristically useless. Without the intervention of the Metis ranch hand, my father would have been badly injured.

I had been doing this cowboy stint every summer since I was fourteen, feeling always disgusted and shamed by the whole thing; I was disgusted by the subculture of defecating cattle, mordant mosquitoes, and noncommunicating (to me) Metis, mysterious earthy strangers from some anthropological field camp. Because I was an extremely bookish child, I could understand nothing I had not read about in books. And because I had read almost no social anthropology, I had no purchase on the French-Indian village world except to loathe and fear it. In my eyes, it was the pit of darkness and ignorance, as it was to my father.

I was very glad that Wednesday before Labor Day in 1951 that my cowboy days would end two days after the holiday. I would get on an overnight coach of the Great Northern Railway for a steamy trip to Minneapolis; then by day coach on the Burlington streamliner to Chicago; then a very long uneasy night on the Pennsylvania Railroad coach with arrival at Trenton at 8:00 A.M. the next day; then by two more local trains finally to Princeton, New Jersey, having traversed backwards half of American history like some alternative universe Lewis and Clark.

I compared my precarious cowboy role, the dung and flies in the bush to imagined serenity and anticipated elegance of the grand old Ivy League university where I would be exactly one week later, commencing my graduate studies toward a Ph.D. in medieval European history. Never again would I have to breathe cow dung. Little did I know that there was an ambiance worse than cow feces.

How did a young Canadian Jewish cowboy come to be headed for Princeton with all expenses paid? By a combination of a Princeton History Department Junior Fellowship and a traveling scholarship from the federated, multicampus University of Manitoba as reward for graduating first in my class in Arts and Science. I eventually turned toward this obscure and difficult field of medieval history after I failed in a coveted summer job between my junior and senior years writing scripts for the awesome state corporation, the CBC News Bureau, in Winnipeg. After five weeks I was fired because the CBC manager told me the news-anchors were in revolt at having to read my heavy, mouth contorting prose. As it was with my horsemanship, so it was with my writing a news script: no one had given me five minutes instruction on how to perform the task, and in this case, I was too naïve and arrogant to teach myself.

On the Canadian prairie, primitive sink or swim capitalism prevailed. I was wounded and humiliated. My parents' head-shaking concern for their unemployable only child confronted me daily like an unwelcome ghost. In desperation I turned to the prospect of an academic career, thinking that with a Ph.D. in history, I might become an impoverished, but dignified, college teacher.

Something happened in October of my senior year to push me southward to Cold War U.S.A., which I, as a rabid Canadian socialist, had up to now despised and imprudently denounced at student conferences. A gold medal was given to the student with the highest cumulative grade point average over the first three years at United College, the component of the University of Manitoba in downtown Winnipeg that I attended. I confidently expected a letter from the college president's office telling me I had won the medal, but on awards night at a cavernous Protestant church, the medal went to Miss Mary Mathers, daughter of the esteemed city coroner.

I went to see the Principal of the college, a United (Presbyterian/Methodist) minister, Reverend Dr. William Creighton Graham, scion of an old Ontarian family. He had been Professor of Old Testament Theology during the thirties at the University of Chicago Divinity School and had published what was in its time a good book on the Hebrew prophets. He was warm and sympathetic as always.

"Dr. Graham," I began aggressively, "there has been a mistake. I should have been awarded the gold medal, not Mary Mathers. I have been in many classes with her and I know my grades in these courses were higher than hers."

"No mistake at all," said the learned Reverend. "We know your average was indeed higher than Mary's."

"Then why didn't I win the medal?" I asked impatiently.

"Because," said Dr. Graham, "the college's Board of Trustees are on my back that Jews, especially you, Norman, keep winning all the academic prizes around here. Frankly, my job was on the line."

I felt like I had been kicked in the stomach. Anger flushed into my face. Dr. Graham was unperturbed. "Haven't we been good to you here at United College, Norman? Haven't you won a full tuition scholarship every year, including this one?"

"Yes, I have."

"Then forget about this little charade of competitive nonsense. Go back to the library and get back to work."

Here was the tough-minded, dryly empirical mind of Scots Presbyterianism at work, making a distinction between the important (spiritual) and unimportant (material) realms. Graham had given me a salutary lesson in Calvinist theology.

I left Graham's office without a word and returned to the college library, which I had haunted day and night for three years. But instead of plowing further through J. H. Clapham's dense *Economic History of Modern Britain*, volume I, a fervent and clever defense of the old market economy, I poked around in a corner of the library stacks and went through the catalog of every Canadian Anglophone university, some twenty of them. I discovered something remarkable. There appeared to be not one name-recognizable Jew teaching history in any Canadian college or university.

I went to see my mentor, J. H. Stewart Reid, the History Department head, a canny Scottish socialist from Toronto. "Dr. Reid, I've been thinking perhaps I should apply to graduate schools of history in the United States instead of going to the University of Toronto next year."

Reid hated the United States with a passion. But now without a second's hesitation he said in a joking, fake Highland accent that he used on special occasions: "Ay, laddie, you should go to the States; they don't like Jews in this country."

I was taken aback. I was certainly not so naïve as to believe that Canada was other than a hotbed of anti-Semitism.

I had gotten beaten up by Ukrainian gangs on my way to school when I was eleven. I knew the Canadian consulates in Europe—under the corrosive influence of the anti-Jewish policies of Prime Minister William Lyon Mackenzie King (1935–48)—turned cartwheels to avoid giving immigration visas to Jewish Holocaust survivors while welcoming Nazis. I knew there were severe quotas limiting the admission of Jews to the University of Manitoba Medical School. I knew that only one Jew, a World War II war hero who had suffered for three years in a Japanese prison camp, had ever been awarded a Rhodes Scholarship to Oxford from Manitoba. I knew that Eaton's department store, Winnipeg's biggest, did not employ Jews even in menial jobs. I knew that it was extremely rare for a Jew to get one of the prized jobs in the Manitoba provincial bureaucracy.

But now the socialist Reid, my idol, had attributed anti-Semitism to Canadian academia in such a jocular and accepting manner. I did not know at that time that Donald Creighton, head of the University of Toronto's flagship History Department—where Reid received his Ph.D.—and a formidable and innovative scholar in Canadian history, was a publicly outspoken anti-Semite like most of the WASP humanists on the Toronto faculty. "But," Reid continued dropping the British music-hall laddie accent, "you can't get a fellowship at a first-rate American graduate school, Norman, in modern European history that you want to pursue. Too many good applicants in that field from distinguished American colleges."

"Then what field should I apply in, Dr. Reid?"

"The Middle Ages," he said chuckling. "There is little competition for student money in that obscure field and a dearth of entering students. I heard just last week that Princeton has three medievalists but only two graduate students in the medieval history field. I know you can read a bit of Latin; you have already mastered French and German. So you have the languages and I will write you a terrific recommendation."

So I applied to Chicago, Princeton, Harvard, and Columbia. Reid was right on target. They all admitted me but only Princeton and Chicago offered money, and Princeton had the best faculty in the medieval field. So that is how I left the unwelcome saddle and arrived at Princeton University in New Jersey at 10:00 A.M. four days after Labor Day 1951, two months before my twenty-second birthday.

My departure for Princeton was very hard on my mother. My father was a remote man who didn't care much where I was—as long as he could be on the ranch with his endearing purebred Hereford cows and the New York Yiddish newspaper he devoured daily (it took most of its articles from the previous day's *New York Times*). But I was an only child and my mother's sole comfort while my father was on his ranch for long stretches. Yet she encouraged me to go to Princeton so I could earn a living and also to impress the affluent and Anglicized among Winnipeg's Jews, who had done very well financially during the War, often by trading in black market goods.

I normally returned to Winnipeg in the summers for only very short visits during my Princeton years, although my parents usually visited me once a year at Princeton on their way to Miami for a month's refuge from the Canadian cold.

The summer of 1956 was different. I spent a whole summer there teaching at the University of Manitoba and at my mother's urging finding a wife among the emerging beauties of Winnipeg Jewry. My first choice turned me down flat to marry a shoe salesman. After a six-week hiatus, my next choice was Mindy, a very attractive, vivacious, and highly intelligent brunet whose parents were distinctly lower middle class—they owned a small coffee shop. On my side it was a love match. Mindy married me because she had reached the ripe old age of twenty-two without any better prospects than me, as her anxious parents and sister daily advised her.

This led to marriage in the summer of 1957; it has turned out to be a very long marriage, more than four decades long. My mother's rich relatives, heretofore celebrating me as the rising academic superstar of the family, now abandoned me because I had married a poor girl from a marginal family.

My son Howard was born in Princeton thirteen months after our marriage; my daughter Judy was born in Manhattan in 1962. The first decade of the marriage was soured by our lack of money and bad housing resulting from the modest salary of a junior academic.

Mindy and my mother did not get on. My mother in her loneliness and anger slid into paranoia and borderline clinical depression. My father took her to the Mayo Clinic in Minnesota for consultation with a psychiatrist. When the psychiatrist started to ask her questions about her sex life, my mother indignantly insisted on going home to Winnipeg.

My father's cattle business was boom or bust. After my marriage, he reported mostly empty pockets and, therefore, the inability to help us financially. I passed into long periods of depression, exacerbating an innate psychological bipolarity I derived from my mother.

❖ 2 ❖

BRITISH
HUMANISM

When I entered college in 1947, Winnipeg, Manitoba, where I lived with my mother ten months a year while my father spent most of his time on his ranch sixty miles away—we three spent the summers together on the ranch—was a city of three hundred thousand people. Its best days economically were drawing to a close although one would never know that from the pages of its staunchly liberal and optimistic newspaper, the *Winnipeg Free Press*. Winnipeg had developed as a railroad hub (both of the transcontinental Canadian railroads had to pass through Winnipeg to get from East to West and they maintained large repair yards there), a meatpacking center (in the St. Boniface stockyards across the river), and above all as a service and manufacturing center for the grain belt in Manitoba and neighboring Saskatchewan.

Winnipeg's greatest days had come in the first two decades of the twentieth century when it was a magnet for East European immigrants, mainly Jews and Ukrainians. But now changing technology and shifting trade patterns were slowly undermining Winnipeg's prosperity with oil discoveries and consequent immigration from the United States, spurring the development of Edmonton and Calgary in Alberta and the growth of Vancouver, British Columbia, as a Pacific port. Winnipeg by 1950 was rapidly losing its Western primacy to these boomtowns.

Today Winnipeg, although its population currently exceeds a half million, is a fiscally depressed city, its once thriving central business district a ghost town and its intellectual life a shadow of what it was in the 1940s. Now the main cultural activity of Winnipeg is sitting at home and watching American cable TV. Today its only cultural lights are the Winnipeg Ballet, founded by British expatriates after the War and still reputable, and the prizewinning, best-selling novelist Carole Shields, an American from the Midwest in origin who got to Winnipeg because her husband teaches at the University there. Shields is currently the chancellor (president of the Board of Trustees) of the state funded University of Winnipeg, which until 1974 was a private Protestant church-supported college, United College, and part of the unwieldy, federated, degree-granting University of Manitoba.

In the 1940s there was a vibrant Yiddish-speaking intellectual life, focused on socialist Zionism, among Winnipeg's Jewish community, who then comprised 10 percent of the city's population (now down to 3 percent). Winnipeg Jewry was a distant but lively outpost of the intense Yiddish intellectual life of Odessa, Warsaw, and the Lower East Side of New York City earlier in the century. All that is gone now. Today the main interest of Winnipeg's Jews is making it to Hawaii or Palm Springs, California, for refuge during the horrible winter months.

My intellectual roots lie anachronistically in the old Yiddish East European culture. I never learned to read Hebrew well but at the age of fourteen, I was writing poetry in Yiddish, having absorbed the whole vast corpus of Yiddish literature. Marxism, Freudianism, and European romanticism and modernism first came to me in the Yiddish language, an expressive German dialect transliterated into the Hebrew alphabet. Trapped in my subconscious was the tempestuous, rebellious, and intellectual world (1880–1925) of the novelist Mendele Mocher Sforim, the poet Haim Nachman Bialik, and the historian Simon Dubnov.

When I entered United College in the fall of 1947, brimming as I was then with socialist Zionist ideology, one still saw in the corridors of the shabby college building faded photographs of late nineteenth-century Presbyterian ministers who founded Manitoba College just as the same kind of intense British Protestants had founded Harvard in the seventeenth century. Early in the twentieth century the Methodist (Wesleyan) church in Winnipeg founded its own Wesley College, a serious educational commitment that was uncommon among the Methodist populists who had split off from the main body of the Anglican Church in the 1790s to service the spiritual needs of the new urban population and impoverished families of the Industrial Revolution.

In the 1920s the Canadian Methodists joined with a majority segment of the country's Presbyterians—a harder and rarer combination than one might think if unversed in Protestant theology. Suffice it to say that the Presbyterians were pessimists about human nature and the Methodists congenital optimists. In spite of their profound differences they joined together to form the unique United Church of Canada.

Thereby Manitoba and Wesley Colleges combined to form the intellectually vibrant, fiscally impoverished United College. But not until the Province of Manitoba took over its funding from the hard-pressed and stingy Protestants in 1974 did the old college on Portage Avenue in downtown Winnipeg, now the public and secular University of Winnipeg, have the authority to grant its own arts and science degrees. In the forties it granted its BA's through the federated University of

Manitoba, whose main campus was in the remote suburb of Fort Gary fittingly on the highway to the U.S. border. Students at the three associated church colleges—Catholic, Anglican, and United—within the University of Manitoba had to take their final exams set at the main campus and actually write these formidable British-style exams in the main campus's gloomy gymnasium.

I went to United College rather than to the main campus of the University strictly for reasons of convenience: I did not drive and getting to the Fort Gary campus from my home required both a trolley and long bus ride out of the Jewish ghetto of North Winnipeg in temperatures that fell to twenty below zero Fahrenheit in winter. United College was only a twenty-minute trolley ride from my home.

United College in the fall of 1947 had eight hundred students, each paying tuition of $200 (about $2,500 in current U.S. dollars). There were about thirty thousand books in the library, four hundred of them the sermons of nineteenth-century Scottish divines. The history collection was nevertheless a good one, and I also had access to the larger collection on the main university campus in Fort Gary. I never went there except to write final exams, but I had friends who were students there and got books out of the University library for me. I remember the excitement in my first year of college when I opened the main campus's copy of Ferdinand Lot's *The End of the Ancient World*, an English translation of the Parisian classic published in 1920. I memorized it, and in the 1960s I used to stun my graduate students by reciting from memory whole paragraphs from it.

In the fall of 1947 there were still a lot of army veterans attending United College under the Canadian equivalent of the G.I. Bill. The campus building could not accommodate this crowd, so large lecture classes were held in a veterans' clubhouse, the Canadian Legion Hall, across Portage Avenue from the college. Until 4:00 P.M. it was a college classroom building; after 4:00 P.M. it was a soldiers' beer hall. The classrooms always smelled of stale malt.

The United College faculty was modestly paid but its quality was high. No one in Winnipeg today, including the University of Winnipeg's chancellor, president, and faculty, seems to have a recollection of what a jewel of a liberal arts college old United was in the late 1940s.

United's head luminary was Carleton Stanley, a distinguished classicist and literary critic who had written books on Sophocles and Matthew Arnold. He came West from Dalhousie University in Halifax, Nova Scotia, where he had been the president. Some said he had retired from administration to go back to teaching; others darkly hinted he had been fired after a dustup with the Dalhousie University Trustees and was teaching at United because he desperately needed the money. He taught the required year-long English literature survey course that began with Chaucer and ended with Matthew Arnold, with a lengthy stop at Shakespeare and Milton along the way. I admired him; he seemed to me to be an embodiment of the best traditions of British humanism. He was an Ontario WASP with a Classics degree from Oxford.

Stanley introduced me to an old, glamorous, and immensely powerful culture, that of British liberal humanism. Without his knowing it in two months he weaned me away from the thin gruel of socialist Zionism in which I had grown up. I withdrew from *Habonim*, the Labor Zionist youth movement in which I had been very active, and stayed home when I was not attending classes and read the books—mountains of them—that Carleton Stanley recommended to his normally over-whelmed class. Each week he would assign a short paper and then he would discuss the three or four best of them—invariably including one of mine—in class. Once he read out loud (without identifying the author) my entire essay on Shakespeare's *Anthony and Cleopatra.* It was an epiphany for me to hear this. I was reborn a new person. No longer a Zionist activist; now a would-be British humanist. I was apotheosized, catapulted into a world of cerebral legend where I felt what the young Ludwig Wittgenstein must have felt around 1910 in Cambridge when Bertrand Russell intoned, "Yes, Wittgenstein, you are a genius."

At 2:00 P.M. every Wednesday Stanley held two hours of open office hours in the same stinking beer hall where he lectured at noon twice a week. He quickly got rid of the other students who came to his office hours and then the two of us sat in the closing afternoon gloom of the True North for ninety minutes and talked of everything from Plato to T. S. Eliot. He had strong opinions about everything. Essentially he was an English Whig, an old-fashioned Edwardian liberal. He treated me as a near equal.

It was the greatest learning experience of my life. I can still see him sitting in his blue high quality but well-worn worsted suit, his unfashionable high top English shoes, his woolen tie and a blue shirt, his gold-rimmed glasses, an unlit pipe dangling from his lips. I have always regarded Carleton Stanley as my first and most important mentor and as a model of what a great teacher ought to be. He taught me to love old England and its law, class system, and literate culture. He gave me enormous personal confidence that I could be like him, a critic and a scholar.

United's English department comprised three professors. This made it a large department in that place and time. Its Philosophy and Economics Departments were each one man operations, but what men they were. Philosophy was taught by David Owens, a Protestant minister with a doctorate in divinity and an M.A. in philosophy from the University of Toronto.

Owens was a native of Winnipeg. He was a neo-Hegelian, which nowadays seems antediluvian but which was in 1947 only about thirty years out-of-date. The Hegelian doctrine was that the only things in the world that were real—permanent—were ideas. Intellectuality determined everything else. In the first decade of the century Hegelian idealism was still strong at Edinburgh, Oxford, Harvard, and Princeton, not to speak of several German universities.

Owens was perpetually discomfited by the head of the Philosophy Department on the University of Manitoba's main campus who set the final exams and was an American pragmatist from Boston, so Owens had to struggle to communicate philosophical systems beyond his beloved Plato, Kant, and Hegel. He had to give due weight to John Dewey and his New Deal philosophy that reality is whatever makes us happy. Yet he did this very well. I used to sit with him during his open office hours while he chewed egg sandwiches with his obtrusive dentures and talked endlessly about the pros and cons of John Dewey's theory, then still the height of intellectual fashion, and which is making a comeback nowadays.

Owens was always shabbily dressed, the cuffs and collars of his perpetual white shirts badly frayed, his suits baggy and not a little dirty. But there was a whole side to him he never revealed to me. Thirty years later, after he was deceased, a cousin of mine in Winnipeg casually mentioned that David Owens had been a pioneering collector of Canadian art of the 1930s and 1940s, then thoroughly unappreciated but later, in the 1960s and 1970s during the nationalist upswing in Canadian culture in the era of Prime Minister Pierre Trudeau, of substantial market value. So poverty-stricken old Reverend Owens left a significant fiscal legacy to his family.

Economics was taught by Gerald Prodrick, a young, intense Torontonian. He hated teaching, especially the introductory course that was obsoletely—for an economics program—on European economic history and that Prodrick, a theoretician (he ended up working as an analyst for a bank) had absolutely no interest in. I learned little economic history from Gerald Prodrick's classes, but I did not have to because the course's textbook, mainly authored by Shepherd B. Clough of Columbia University's History Department, the *Economic History of Europe*, was so good. It encapsulated all the important new work of the 1930s and 1940s in economic history done in Britain, the United States, and the Continent and deeply enriched my historical understanding.

From it I got a sense for the first time of the immense structural complexity of European history: important scholarly names like John U. Neff, R. H. Tawney, Eli Hecksher, Henri Pirenne, Michael Postan, and John H. Clapham became familiar to me. To Prodrick's surprise —and perhaps dismay—I went to the library after absorbing Clough's fascinating textbook and read the masterpieces by these great historians that Clough had mentioned. Thirteen years later I found myself a tenured associate professor in the Columbia History Department with Shep Clough's office five doors down the hall from mine. I told him one day that his textbook had made me a historian. He quizzically looked at me in embarrassment and disbelief.

What I got from Prodrick was not economics but an introduction to art film. His passion was the European films of the 1930s and 1940s, completely unknown in Winnipeg. Prodrick devoted most of his time to organizing and running the College Film Society, whose showings of

Eisenstein, Jean Renoir, early Hitchcock, etc., I devotedly attended. There was nothing more important in my college education, except for the informal tutorials with Carleton Stanley and David Owens.

The United College History Department, like its English Department, was a relatively large one. Besides the wily Stewart Reid, the head, it consisted of Kenneth McNaught, an upper-class socialist from Toronto, and Tryggve J. Oleson, a medievalist who was a native of Winnipeg with a Ph.D. from Toronto. There Oleson studied with the prominent German Catholic medievalist (later at UCLA) Gerhardt Ladner. Oleson was a passionate Roman Catholic convert from the Icelanders' traditional Lutheranism. He felt uncomfortable in the United College bastion of Protestantism and by the time I reached my senior year he held an appointment in the main campus of the University, where I continued to study with him. He was not very good in the classroom but he was a man of prodigious learning and high promise who died young from a stroke. His son is today one of the editors of the *Winnipeg Free Press*.

Kenneth McNaught taught Canadian and U.S. history. In the fall of 1947 I listened (I never took class notes in college) to his lectures on U.S. history in the stinking beer hall. It was mainly Charles Beard, the New York leftist of the thirties, but with an add-on of the latest monographs. McNaught went on to become a leading professor at the University of Toronto and to write the *Penguin History of Canada*, the all-time best-selling survey of Canadian history—and ideologically much more moderate than McNaught's personal views.

In the mid-1990s I wrote to him at his elegant country home to which he had by then retired and recalled his first college class that I had witnessed in the United beer hall in the fall of 1947. I pointed out that in that room there was another future best-selling historian, namely me, then a gawky and pushy Jew who wrote *The Civilization of the Middle Ages*. Would anyone in 1947 have imagined that among the young, nervous, thin, almost anorexic assistant professor and his 100 green students absorbing the American Civil War that fall there were two future best-selling historians in respectively Canadian and medieval fields? Of course not, least of all Canadians who imagined that important writers of history exist only in Britain or the United States.

McNaught thanked me for my letter in 1996 and the autographed paperback copy of my book that accompanied it but made no comment on my picture of the hoary 1947 scene in the Canadian Legion Hall on Portage Avenue. Ken hated Winnipeg as a barbarian place and perhaps preferred to forget it all. I have not. I still ruminate on a gray, frigid postwar November morning, McNaught at the podium, his head down, reading his lecture, his rigid Marxism coated with good information from the sources beyond the flaming Charles Beard.

A half block down Portage Avenue from the college in the late 1940s there was a very good bookstore that featured the Penguin classics, then starting to pour from the press, and some current British hardcover history books. I remember plunking down $4, a steep price, to buy a newly arrived copy in 1950 of A. L. Rowse's *The England of Elizabeth*, a beautiful and underappreciated book by that quirky Cornishman and Oxford don.

Distant as Winnipeg was from Picadilly Circus in the late 1940s I could reasonably feel that the Canadian prairie city was directly connected to the cultural as well as the political centers of the British Empire-Commonwealth. During the War, once a week in school we stood up and after *God Save the King* and *O Canada* we sang to the music of Edward Elgar's *Pomp and Circumstance March no. 1*: "Land of Hope and Glory, / Mother of the Free, / How shall we extol thee, / Who are born of thee? / Wider still and wider / Shall thy bounds be set, / God who made thee mighty, / Make thee mightier yet."

I thought I had a special right to sing these words because my favorite uncle, my mother's half-brother, who had lived in our home for two years as a surrogate elder brother, had died fighting as a First Lieutenant in the British Army in Belgium on September 9, 1944, at the age of twenty-three, felled by a German sniper's bullet as he crossed the Albert Canal.

But my Anglophilism was something deeper and more structural than that. I believed in British culture and the general beneficence of the British Empire. Of course I was not blind, considering my socialist Zionist background, to the defects and limitations of the British Empire. Of course I could spout—but I no longer believed in—John Hobson's and V. I. Lenin's theory that imperialism was the final, most decadent, thoroughly vicious stage of capitalism. On Stewart Reid's recommendation I read E. M. Forster's *Passage to India*, the 1922 highly prophetic picture of the British Raj in India and by implication elsewhere as doomed. But I came away from the book with a reaction that Reid—or Forster—had not anticipated.

How sad it was that the Indians did not appreciate the benefits of English law, education, and technology even if the Raj treated them as second-class citizens, like Jews in Canada. Even when the Brits were obtuse and arrogant they really meant well, I believed. Paradoxically David Lean's 1983 film of Forster's novel suggests this subtext as well, indicating perhaps that now that we are in the postimperial era and the British look silly and weak, we can after all acknowledge the good and brave things they accomplished overseas.

I firmly believed in the 1940s, under Carleton Stanley's tutelage, that if Britain, led by a heir of the old aristocracy, Winston Churchill, had not summarily refused Hitler's generous peace terms in the summer of 1940, the Nazi hordes would have taken over the world, even the over-confident United States. I have seen no reason since then to change this judgment. With all that was class-ridden, anti-intellectual, exploitative, smug, even racist about the old Brits, they were relatively speaking the salt of the earth, the best mankind had to offer. "Never have so many owed so much to so few," in the words of Churchill's encomium on the Royal Air Force of 1940.

There are two fundamental things to say about the old culture that dominated the Anglophone universities in 1950. First, it was a print culture; it lived and perpetuated itself by words in written texts. Secondly, it was largely a heritage of the Victorian British (and mainly English) upper middle class. At the margins there were French, German, Italian, and even American contributions, but it was a British episteme, or discourse, or thought-world, or cultural structure.

That it should have become unraveled and diminished in the following six decades as Britain became powerless, impoverished, and bewildered is not surprising. Every high culture needs a political core to fasten onto. As Britain's political power vanished, the humanistic culture gathered around it was greatly damaged. It gave way to a newer post modernist culture influenced more by Paris than Oxbridge and London, which reached its high point in the campuses of the American university after the expansion and upheavals of the sixties.

The old culture was severely diminished in its social power by the challenge of the new oral and non-linear visual media driving a post-

Gutenberg galaxy, beginning with television and rock music also in the 1960s. This latter development was keenly prophesized in the 1950s book by a University of Toronto English professor and sociologist Marshall McLuhan, developing ideas delineated by the Saint Louis University Jesuit philosopher Walter Ong and the Canadian economic historian Harold Innis.

From the time McLuhan propounded his doctrine that "the medium is the message" (he later said, "the massage") and American TV (whose content McLuhan disliked) was the harbinger of a neo-oral culture, I thought he was on the right track. He was, by the way, another oddball communicator to come out of the vibrant atmosphere of the University of Manitoba in the forties.

The roots of the British Victorian humanistic culture that was still propagated at United College in the late 1940s lie in the English common law, classical philosophy (Plato, Aristotle, Locke, Hume, and Kant mostly), the ideology and behavior pattern of the gentry (the rural upper middle class), and in Christian ethics as developed by the medieval Church and further refined by Scottish Calvinism and given a secular overlay by the French and American Enlightenments.

It contained ingredients that could be used to justify imperialism and class hierarchy and also to condemn them. It could be molded into the Tory conservatism of Disraeli and Margaret Thatcher but also into the social democracy of the British Labor party and its cognates in Anglophone countries (Canadian and Australian socialism; Keynesian economics and the American New Deal), as well as John Dewey's progressive pragmatism.

Because British humanistic culture was so malleable and plastic, it was bound to be shredded by the political and social conflicts of the

Cold War era and the capitalist expansion of the later twentieth century, a shredding given ideological focus by the New Left of the sixties
and the cultural revolution of the non-linear television, rock, and information age.

Neo-conservatives today yearn for British humanism's reconstitu-
tion because of its stability, plasticity, civility, and respect for education,
learning, and carefully measured meritorious careers open to talent and
hard work.

The old humanistic culture was, however, more a blend, a com-
pendium of ideas and attitudes joined together over many centuries than
a clearly articulated theory, and it was therefore bound to be found
wanting by many academics who came along during and after the upheavals of the 1960s.

Around 1860 the English critic, poet, and school inspector Matthew Arnold tried to articulate a theory of liberal humanism. It didn't
work; he sounded pompous, didactic, and disjointed. A century later
the American critic and Columbia University literature professor, Lionel
Trilling, tried to do the same thing. Although much praised by the New
York City *literati* at the time, Trilling's effort had no staying power. He
sounded hesitant, overcautious, and defensive. Perhaps it cannot be
done. Maybe British humanism is more a personal code and mind-set
and a complex historical tradition than a theory of social action. The
leftist American professors after 1968 disdained it and the neo-
conservatives now nostalgically adore it.

The attractiveness of a cultural theory such as British humanism is
not exclusively built upon its intellectual consistency. Neither Nazism
nor Soviet Communism made much sense in abstract theoretical terms,
but they certainly inspired enormous devotion until brought down by
military defeat in the former case and economic collapse in the latter.

Yet it is worth noting that British humanism, which functioned as establishmentarian culture of the Anglophone academia in the middle of the twentieth century, did contain an inherent structural flaw. It was based both on contemporary exercise of reasoning and also upon historical tradition. It assumed that these two highly diverse sources would meld and integrate with each other into a solid and seamless cultural system.

T. S. Eliot was an important early twentieth-century cultural theorist, in spite of his gimcrack religiosity and bitter anti-Semitism, because he offered assurance in a loud and clear voice that reason and history converged in support of validating British humanism. But reason might be pulled by the emerging behavioral sciences into contrary directions, and a more learned and sophisticated reading of history might raise grave questions about the moral imperative of the English past's legacy to the present. This is what happened after 1960.

In the 1760s William Blackstone in his *Commentaries on the Laws of England* ran into precisely this problem when he claimed the old common law was validated both by Enlightenment reason and by evolving historical structures that ended at the same point of ethical validation. In the 1780s the utilitarian legal thinker Jeremy Bentham, a man without illusions and sentiment, called Blackstone's double validation of the common law in which reason and history were alleged to deliver the same message to be "nonsense on stilts." The academic generation that came to the fore after 1968 had a similar dyspeptic view of British humanism as an academic culture.

There was yet another problem with the old culture. There was a world of difference between when it was a relatively passive guardian of customary ways of teaching and learning on college campuses and when it was subjected to the polarizing, heated ambience of the 1950s and

1960s. It may have seemed fussy and a bit boring in the old days but it was tolerable, even persuasive in a Mr. Chips sort of way. But when British humanism came to be refashioned in the fifties as an aggressive instrument of the Cold War, its inherent contradictions and marginal weaknesses became glaringly evident and the post-1968 radical academic generation capitalized on this awkward vulnerability.

British humanism as a cultural theory was comforting and looked admirable in a context of Victorian Empire, common law traditions, gentrification and social hierarchy, and excellent schooling for a small minority. Cast into the harsh, ambitious, competitive, democratic world of Cold War America it began to decompose and shrivel.

This is a fact that today burns the neo-conservatives. It was as much the overextension and misdirection of British humanism into an instrument of global politics by its friends that damaged it from within as the assault upon it from the Marxists, Freudians, and postmodernist deconstructionists from the outside.

In my first semester of college teaching at Princeton in the fall of 1955, I was assigned to help out in an interdepartmental introductory course on the humanities in Western Civilization. The course was taught by Paul Ramsey, a prominent Protestant theologian and head of the Religion Department, and Anthony Raubitschek, a classical philosopher of standing. Their lectures were excellent and their command of the most recent learning exemplary. But as the semester wore on, I saw the weakness in what they were doing.

They drew a rigid paradigm of how classical and biblical thought had united in late antiquity and in the medieval Church, and it was this neo-Thomist "synthesis" that the United States stood for in the Cold War. They believed that the critical moment in Western thought came in the thirteenth century when St. Thomas Aquinas integrated, it was claimed, the diverse biblical and classical traditions. They saw the United States as the direct heir of this Western synthesis. This idea was very popular in the Ivy League and at the University of Chicago in the 1950s.

This was not entirely wrong, but it was crude, oversimplified, and historically doubtful. As young as I was, I rebelled against it and in effect undermined it when they asked me to give a lecture on St. Augustine of Hippo (d. 430). I focused on Augustine's powerful sex drive and, as a native North African, his contempt for Rome, and his authoritarian belief in the use of violence against heretical Christian minorities. This did not sound like President Dwight Eisenhower and his pious Secretary of State, John Foster Dulles. I was not invited back to teach in this course. Raubitschek, an angry man, excoriated me for my intellectual waywardness.

Called upon by the Emperor Augustus around 10 A.D. to defend the new Roman Empire established by murder, slavery, and deceit, his court poet, the gentleman farmer Virgil, wrote a very long epic but offered limited and cautious encomia for Rome's conquest and pillage of the whole Mediterranean world. The Roman leadership cadre were descended somehow from the old Trojans whom the Greeks had beaten in the Trojan War—some glory!—said Virgil. Rome did not promise prosperity and happiness but merely peace: the purpose of the Empire, said Virgil, was "to spare the humble and crush the proud" and it certainly at least did the latter. Virgil, in the *Aeneid* at any rate, took a modest and cautious approach to validating Roman power morally.

So for a long time did Victorians as well with respect to the British Empire, but the messianic strains of "Land of Hope and Glory" showed by the early twentieth century something more hysterical was going on. When Britain crashed into military ignominy, poverty and fiscal crisis, and wasteful socialism by 1950, it was the United States that in the Cold War 1950s took up the messianic beat and pushed British humanism beyond its former ambivalent and relatively modest role as an academic culture and thereby helped mightily to discredit it.

Virgil was a wise man. Ideological triumphalism is self-defeating. The more an established culture lays claim to ethical superiority, the more vulnerable it becomes to its critics. This was how the 1950s prepared the way for intellectual rebellion in the 1960s.

❖ 3 ❖

THE CULMINATION
OF THE OLD CULTURE

B efore my arrival at the Graduate College (residence for graduate students) at Princeton in the first week of September 1951, I, the Canadian cowboy, had been once in the eastern United States. I had spent the summer of 1949 attending the "Institute of World Affairs" in the Connecticut Berkshires, a six-week summer program for thirty students from around the world paid for by a Quaker woman phil-anthropist. A student in the summer before me at this Institute was Henry Kissinger from Harvard. The director of the program in 1949 was a right-wing politics professor from Harvard, William Y. Elliot. This was the first time I encountered a renowned academic who was also a conservative, and Elliot made me stop and think and helped me move from socialism to at least the moderate center.

Before and after the six-week world affairs seminar, I spent a week in New York City. The Camel cigarette sign blowing smoke on Times Square, a Dodgers-Cardinal game at Ebbets Field, and the palatial Fifth Avenue apartment of the Quaker woman as well as the museums are what I remember. New York in 1949 was mostly still unair-conditioned and the subway trains were filthy, but it was a safe city.

Every time now I take a train from Grand Central, I remember that city as thirty 19- and 20-year-old college students headed by rail for a prep school in Salisbury, Connecticut, where the summer institute was held and where Wild Bill Elliot harangued us for six weeks about how good a thing NATO was, something I never heard at United College. The supposed high point of the seminar was when Eleanor Roosevelt came and spoke in her high-pitched voice. I found her a redundant voice from the past.

That summer I visited not only the imperial campus of Columbia University with Stanford White's majestic buildings, but also the campus of Yale in New Haven, about sixty miles from the summer seminar site.

When I got to Princeton, New Jersey, on that September morn in 1951, I was surprised how different Princeton University was physically—and I soon learned institutionally—from not only Columbia but even Yale. Princeton's campus was small and bucolic in a well-trimmed way; it was like living on a golf course. The only significant buildings were the chapel, a Gothic structure modest in size built around 1930; the Firestone Library, opened in 1950 after a gift from the tire czar (the library was cleverly built in lateral steps into the side of a sloping hill and had open stacks, completely accessible to all students); the Chancellor Green Library, by 1951 transformed into a messy student center with a cafeteria, a splendid later nineteenth-century H. H. Richardson American Romanesque structure right out of a Henry James or Edith Wharton novel, with walls so thick it could have resisted an artillery attack; and the Graduate College on the edge of the campus. The latter featured a tower grandiosely modeled on and exaggerating that of

Magdalen College, Oxford. "Oxford by Cecil B. DeMille," an émigré British graduate student called it.

For two of my three years as a student in residence at the Graduate College where all residents dined in long black choir gowns on Howard Johnson cuisine, I shared a small two-room suite with an American history graduate student from the Carolinas, Tom Clark. He went on to graduate from Harvard Law School and became an attorney for Dupont in Wilmington, Delaware. In the 1990s Tom ran a Sunday night lecture series in an Episcopalian Church, funded by a Dupont heiress, and invited me down annually five times to lecture on sundry historical subjects. Tom Clark gives this picture of me when he first reached our suite a day after me: at 7:00 A.M. I was sitting in an armchair, dressed in a coat, shirt and tie, smoking a pipe, and reading a book on medieval history—in German—that I had gotten out of the Firestone Library. I don't know how he tolerated me for two years as a roommate; neither does he in retrospect.

On my third day in Princeton I took the language exams in German, French, and Latin and passed all three—the German with ease because of my deep knowledge of Yiddish; the French and Latin barely. I immediately realized that in spite of five years of Latin in school and two in college, my Latin was only minimally satisfactory for graduate work and research in medieval history. I loved to read German and I spent some off-hours in my student years at Princeton translating the lyric poems of Walther von der Vogelweide, who wrote in the early thirteenth century. I managed to scrape by in French, which I was required to study for six miserable years in school in bilingual Canada and which I hated—having to read one half of *Les Misérables* in the original will do that. But Latin was a big stumbling block.

Latin and I were never comfortable with each other. I have always refused to administer the Latin language exam to my graduate students on the grounds that it would be deceitful because my own Latin barely passed muster. But on the other hand, I discovered in five years as assistant to the greatest American medieval historian, Joseph R. Strayer, that his Latin was no better than mine. Strayer could read with ease a royal government document but had great trouble with high ecclesiastical Latin. He simply avoided it by not working on the medieval church. I have been comforted by the fact that Archbishop Thomas Becket, the Canterbury martyr, a college dropout, couldn't read or write ecclesiastical Latin. His secretary, the classical scholar John of Salisbury, did it for him.

In my first year at Princeton I had assignments of thirty pages of thick ecclesiastical Latin a week from Theodor E. Mommsen, who was my mentor as well as teacher. Fortunately, another first year student, William M. Bowsky, a classics graduate of NYU, was there to assist me. Together we labored over the Latin assignments each week. I reciprocated by teaching Bowsky history, which at the beginning he hardly knew. Bowsky became a leading historian of the government and society of Renaissance Italy, especially Siena. In 1998 a special academic conference was held at Stanford University in his honor. Bowsky's first wife was a vivacious Florentine countess whom he married while he was a Fulbright Scholar researching in the chaotic Italian archives. That was a social promotion for a Jewish boy from Washington Heights in upper Manhattan, as the Princeton faculty remarked. The Florentine countess, however, turned out to be impecunious. She claimed that her whole trousseau went down on the Andrea Doria.

In spite of Tom Clark discovering me in sartorial elegance—or so I thought—on the first day he met me in our suite at the Graduate

College, my biggest problem in my first week at Princeton was, in fact, clothes. On my fourth day at the University I was sitting in the History Study Room in the Firestone Library when Jerome Blum, the historian of the Russian peasantry, and one of the two and one-half Jews out of 20 on the history faculty (this made the Department under its Chairman Joe Strayer wildly liberal; the Princeton English Department had no Jewish faculty and if it could manage it, no Jewish graduate students) invited me for a chat in the hall. I obeyed.

"Are you going to the track today, Cantor?" Blum said.

"The track?"

"Yes, racetrack. That jacket you are wearing with the loud checks and that garish tie make you look like a racetrack tout. You won't be around here long, Cantor, unless you get some Ivy League clothes."

I said nothing. I did not tell Jerry Blum how much cattle dung my father, the very model of a Canadian boondocks gentleman, had to eat to get the money to send me off to Princeton.

I left Firestone and stumbled along the main street of the town, Nassau Street. There were plenty of men's clothing stores catering to this all-male university with fashionable gray tweed jackets and dark stripe suits, but the posted prices in the windows were staggering. Finally I came to the last clothing store on Nassau Street, Harry Ballot and Co. The clothes displayed in the window looked appropriately Princeton and the prices were a little more moderate than at Langrock's and the other gentlemen's clothiers. I looked into the shop. It was empty except for a man in his sixties in his shirtsleeves, leaning back in a chair and chewing on a toothpick. He was a very Jewish-looking person. This was presumably Harry Ballot himself.

I entered and in tears told Harry my predicament. He smiled. "Not to worry, boychick; I fix you up. I give you a whole new wardrobe like the Tiger gentlemen. You pay me back in installments. Fifty dollars a month." When I left the store an hour later, I owed Harry $700, but I had the necessary wardrobe.

Four months later, another first year graduate student in medieval history, the Californian Robert L. Benson, accused me of being "a clotheshorse." On every possible occasion I paraded in my Ivy clothes in front of Jerry Blum (he was the resident Master of the Graduate College and presided over every dinner in the elaborate oak paneled dining room). He said nothing further about my dress. Perhaps his devastating warning had been a kind of hazing, although he himself—a bachelor, never to be married—was a sharp dresser, perhaps to help disguise his thick Baltimore Jewish accent.

Besides Jerry Blum the other full-blooded Jew in the History Department was Elmer Beller, the scion of a wealthy eastern U.S. German Jewish family. He had graduated from Princeton in the thirties, had taken a doctorate in history at Oxford, had fought in the War as a captain, and had lost a leg in battle. He lived with his clever wife on a sprawling estate about ten miles from Princeton; they had no children. Beller published little and was only a mediocre teacher, but he was important to the Department because he brought to it the wealth and social position that characterized half the undergraduates.

Beller was important in another way. His palatial home was the site each Thursday of the weekly poker games over which Joe Strayer presided. Unless you participated in these poker matches, you were an outsider in the Department. Once in 1958 when I was an assistant professor I was invited to the Thursday game. Then to Joe Strayer's disgust it was discovered that I didn't know how to play poker—my parents thought playing cards was a sin. I was not invited back. This

wipeout on the poker circuit at the Beller estate was one reason I failed
to get tenure at Princeton in 1960.

Mrs. Beller fixed me up for a date with a Jewish economist at
Rutgers in New Brunswick, New Jersey, fifteen miles away. Because I
couldn't drive, I had to arrive by bus for the date, making a poor
impression on the young woman two years older than me. She was a
graduate of upper crust Smith College. Her father was a wealthy Boston
pharmacist. She humiliated me by demonstrating that her Latin was
actually better than mine, not to mention mathematics. No romance
could sprout in such rocky soil. She was the only young woman I met
during my three years in residence as a graduate student at Princeton.

Not that there weren't attractive young women about on weekends.
There were hundreds of them. They poured off the train on Friday
afternoon, the weekend dates of the undergraduates. The women were
70 percent blondes. In winter they all wore camel hair coats, then very
expensive commodities. There were dozens of bed-and-breakfasts in the
town that lived off the undergraduates' dates—it was still against the
rules for women to sleep in the male students' dormitory beds, although
it was done aplenty.

I salivated watching these women from the Seven Sisters colleges
parading on Nassau Street or entering and leaving the posh eating clubs
(autonomous fraternities) on Prospect Street. They were goddesses as
remote from me as Athena or Venus. I swore to myself that one day, as
a rising Ivy League faculty star, I would have one. It didn't happen. In
May I would sit for hours near the tennis courts watching these bronzed

young women playing tennis with their dates, frequently with a beer can or a cocktail glass in their hands. St. Laurent, Manitoba, was a galaxy far, far away.

My problem socially was that my taste in women always ran to tall blondes from rich families—wherever I lived—but I never could bring myself to approach these goddesses. I was a reasonably handsome but swarthy, big-nosed Jew with no money. Instead of one of those tall, blonde, rich *shiksas* in a camel hair coat I witnessed getting off the train at the Princeton Station, I married a Jewish girl from Winnipeg who was good-looking and slim, who became well educated, a good mother, and an excellent cook. But she was short, dark-haired, and poor. This was not the way to sexual satisfaction and marital bliss.

I suppose I should have snuck onto the University's tennis courts in the summer of 1952 and between sets asked one of the blonde goddesses from Mount Holyoke, Smith, or Vassar whether she was interested in dating a now pudgy, swarthy, impecunious Jewish Medievalist. I thought about doing that or something like it persistently for three years but I lacked the nerve. And so it was back to my study carrel in the basement of the Firestone Library to read papal bulls or thirteenth-century tax rolls. Incessant work was the outlet for my strong sex drive. I was a walking example of Freud's theory of sublimation.

There was one other history professor who was part Jewish by birth, Eric Goldman. He came from the slums of Baltimore and had been virtually adopted while an undergraduate on a scholarship at Johns Hopkins by Frederick C. Lane, the Department chair and an outspoken

New Deal liberal who was the world's greatest expert on Renaissance shipping. Goldman took a Ph.D. in twentieth-century U.S. history at Hopkins and then went to work at *Time* magazine. In 1947 he somehow came to the attention of Joe Strayer, as chairman ever scouting for brilliant young men who might make popular teachers.

Goldman taught the most heavily enrolled course at Princeton. It was limited to 450 students because that was the largest lecture room on the campus. Goldman was always short of "preceptors" (teaching assistants) for his course to lead the discussion sections (preceptorials) while he lectured twice a week to standing room only crowds. In 1958 he was so desperate for backup that he got Strayer to make me one of his preceptors. He was surprised that I knew quite a bit about modern U.S. history—thanks to my socialist youth and to Kenneth McNaught's instruction at United College. Goldman was through and through a New Deal Democrat, much to the left of the majority of the students, who nevertheless admired him.

From attending his lectures I soon learned why. Eric was the best college lecturer I ever encountered. He showed that one can be a stand-up comic and still impart deep learning to students, or rather that the jokes—including a devastating imitation of Harry Truman—helped the students understand the serious stuff. Especially illuminating to me was his famous lecture early in his course on "The Importance of 'Alexander's Ragtime Band' [an early Irving Berlin song and the excuse for a wonderful late-1930s film] in American history." It was a stupendous piece of cultural history. Each year the lecture resulted in a standing ovation. Goldman deserved it. I now aimed to model myself on Eric Goldman as a teacher. I threw away my painfully written out lectures on the early Middle Ages and spoke extemporaneously. I burlesqued Constantine and Charlemagne. I told funny risqué stories about monks and bishops. I hammed it up as a fierce and dumb Viking. I assumed the role of the radical pope, Gregory VII.

From obscurity I soon found myself celebrated on the front page of the *Daily Princetonian* in their annual faculty evaluation issue as one of the seven best lecturers on the campus. Joe Strayer was stunned. He thought—perhaps wrongly—that I had the makings of a prodigious scholar but he had doubted that I would ever do much in the classroom. My striking success, however, in emulation of Eric Goldman, aroused jealousy from some of the senior department faculty and also contributed to my not getting tenure in 1960. Also the success went to my head and I became reckless in my remarks about departmental and university matters, which distressed Uncle Joe Strayer. I got up and spoke in monthly meetings of the whole faculty, a no-no in Strayer's eyes. I had the temerity to give an interview to the *Daily Princetonian.*

Eric Goldman's private life was not a happy one. In New York he had married a beautiful and delicate-looking woman who was a concert pianist of some promise. She did not adjust well to the stultifying Princeton environment, which was harsh on intelligent and well-educated faculty wives. Goldman's wife deteriorated into schizophrenia. Yet he remained very loyal to her and took care of his now psychotic invalid wife for several decades, turning down invitations to give his celebrated lectures on other campuses so that he could be with her daily.

The faculty I came to know best were my teachers: three members of the Department—Strayer; Theodor Mommsen the Younger (T. E. Mommsen to distinguish him from his awesome grandfather, Theodor Mommsen the Elder, the all-time best historian of ancient Rome); and the Renaissance historian E. Harris (Jinks) Harbison. In my circuit were

also the art historian Kurt Weitzmann, a great Byzantinist, and Mommsen's friend Ernst Kantorowicz (EKA) at the Institute for Advanced
Study at the other end of Tigertown five miles away.

In 1951 Princeton University was still primarily an undergraduate
college. There were only a handful of distinguished graduate programs,
mainly physics, mathematics, history, and art history that had developed
since the late 1930s under the impetus of the Institute for Advanced
Study, in turn founded, with Bamberger department store money, as a
refuge for Albert Einstein and other German-Jewish scientists and
scholars, and not part of the University. The History Department under
Joe Strayer's chairmanship aimed to be world class, especially in European history and had reached that level. But in the early 1950s the
history faculty were still not paid to teach graduate students; they did
that on their own time, not as part of their recognized teaching load.

The all-important thing was to teach the young undergraduate
gentlemen, at least half of whom were from the South. Princeton had
always been known as the northernmost southern university since its
founding in the eighteenth century and still was in the 1950s. This
perhaps explains its prowess then on the football field. In 1952 it was
rated fourth in the whole country and football became such a campus
mania that the administration and trustees decided to de-emphasize the
game by prohibiting football scholarships and spring practice.

Undergraduate social life was dominated by the eating clubs on
Prospect Street. Each spring these clubs for upperclassmen decided
which sophomores to admit to their membership. The eating clubs only

had room for 95 percent of the sophomore class. The unselected 5 percent, mostly Jews, were shunted off to a Spartan dining hall named appropriately after Woodrow Wilson.

When he was President of Princeton in the first decade of the century, Wilson announced that he intended to revolutionize the Tigertown ambience by closing down the eating clubs and also by resisting the building of a separate Graduate College. He wanted the graduate students to live in undergraduate dorms and serve as role models and mentors to the young gentlemen from Virginia, Georgia, etc.

Wilson was defeated on both counts by the alumni and the trustees. He left to become Governor of New Jersey for the corrupt Democratic machine and then was elected President in 1912 when the Republican party split apart. He was reelected in 1916 by the narrowest of margins by promising to keep the United States out of the Great War in Europe. A few months later he persuaded Congress to declare war on Germany. Although touted now as the great father figure of modern Princeton, the irascible and stubborn Wilson, a fervent ideologist, was in fact hated and feared by students and faculty alike and driven from the presidency by the trustees.

Whether Princeton would have been a better place in the 1950s if Wilson had carried out his liberal reforms is hard to say. The eating clubs are still there but nowadays 20 percent of the students choose not to become members of one. The Graduate College still sits by itself overlooking a golf course, which is much too expensive for all but a handful of graduate students to use.

Under the aegis of Strayer, Mommsen, Harbison, and Weitzmann, and with some contact with Kantorowicz, I flourished in my three years residence as a student. I put on twenty pounds in my first year; the caterer at the Graduate College, Howard Johnson, cooked much better than my mother. I mastered all aspects of the Middle Ages intimately and burrowed ever deeper into the old culture of British humanism. But I found no lover, not even a datable girlfriend in that still single-sex community.

I was appointed at the end of my second year to the Porter Ogden Jacobus Fellowship, awarded to the student considered best in the whole graduate student population of six hundred students. Considering the supersonic geniuses in the Physics and Mathematics Departments, that took some lobbying by Joe Strayer.

Years later during the 1960s and 1970s when I had a falling out with the now Marxist-dominated Princeton History Department, the ruling group in the faculty there made me an "unperson" as an alumnus by refusing to mention any of my accomplishments in the Department's graduate alumni newsletter. For this kind of long-standing abuse, the President of the University in the early 1990s, Harold Shapiro, personally apologized to me.

In 1954–55 I spent a dreadful year at Oxford on a Rhodes Scholarship. I had been selected as Junior Fellow of the Harvard Society of Fellows, on Strayer and Mommsen's nomination—and was slated to go there in the summer of 1955, when in April I got a terse cable from Joe Strayer. Mommsen had resigned to go to Cornell and Strayer offered me a tenure-track instructorship to teach Mommsen's course on the early Middle Ages (from late Antiquity to 1100 A.D.) and to be Strayer's perpetual teaching assistant in his two courses on the High Middle Ages (1100–1350) and English Constitutionalism and Common Law to 1689. The Harvard Fellowship was intrinsically more rewarding than the Princeton appointment—at Harvard I could do anything I wanted and travel anywhere for three years and also get paid a little more than the Princeton job, which carried a heavy teaching load of fourteen hours a week. Yet I responded positively to Strayer.

The academic job market was still in its postwar depression. I tried for a job at Bryn Mawr and was abruptly repulsed because I was a Jew and not married and, therefore, a threat to the college maidens. A good teaching job might be hard to find after three years in the lotus land of the Harvard Society of Fellows. In addition, the talk around the History Department was always that while I might become a hotshot scholar (this didn't happen) I would be only a mediocre and unpopular teacher (this also didn't happen—so much for prognostication on graduate students' later careers, no more reliable than flipping a coin). I wanted as soon as possible to test myself in the classroom. I also took the Princeton job because it was obvious Joe Strayer wanted me to do so.

Joseph Strayer was the son of George Strayer, a prominent professor at Columbia University Teachers College and a close associate of John Dewey. Joe physically resembled his father—strong, stocky men with big heads. The family was Pennsylvania Dutch (i.e., German) in origin and fiercely dedicated to learning and social improvement. Joe's younger brother, Paul, an economist, also taught at Princeton until his premature death from cancer. Joe lived on into his mid-eighties.

Joe hated growing up on Columbia's Morningside Heights in the 1920s nor did he have good things to say about the excellent Horace Mann prep school in Riverdale the Bronx that he attended. He flourished as an undergraduate at Princeton and was attracted to the Middle Ages by Dana C. Munro, a pioneering scholar on the Crusades. Munro produced a mediocre textbook on medieval history, which Joe during the 1940s extensively rewrote as Strayer and Munro; the textbook went through five editions.

It was characteristic of Joe's loyalty that he kept Munro's name on the book even though by its fourth edition there was almost none of the Munro original flaccid writing in it; it was also characteristic that the book should be very strong on political and very weak on religious and cultural history. St. Augustine of Hippo is dismissed in a few unsympathetic lines!

Strayer like at least half the American medieval historians of his generation got his Ph.D. at Harvard with Charles Homer Haskins, whose prime disciple he turned out to be. Haskins, from an upper-middle-class Pennsylvania family, started out in U.S. history, but he abandoned that to go to Europe and use up his family's money to undergo training in France as a medievalist and spend several years pursuing the accomplishments of the Norman French "supermen" as Haskins called them, in France, England, and Sicily.

Haskin's publications and favorable reputation in France got him a professorship at Harvard. He succeeded Charles Gross, the English Jew and a pioneering scholar on medieval guilds who had been appointed under the liberal Harvard presidency of Charles W. Eliot. After Haskins entered the Harvard History Department, no Jew during his regime there, which lasted into the early 1930s, was appointed.

Haskins was an academic imperialist or "patron" as they say in France in the grand manner. He founded the establishmentarian, intellectually conservative Medieval Academy of America and its journal *Speculum*, and he also served with distinction as Dean of the Graduate School of Arts and Science at Harvard. He was one of two principal academic advisers to Woodrow Wilson at the Versailles Peace Conference and was thus partly responsible for Yugoslavia's creation.

Haskins' academic imperialism was also exhibited in the pressure he brought to insert his Ph.D.s into entry level jobs at leading universities, such as Gaines Post at Wisconsin and Strayer at Princeton. Haskins chose, from his array of brilliant graduate students, Charles H. Taylor to succeed him at Harvard, which was a big mistake: Taylor's scholarship was modest both in quality and quantity. He never published a major book. Yet Strayer and Taylor remained forever close allies. They even published a little book together, a very dull book on medieval French taxation.

In my first year of graduate studies at Princeton, I was haunted and terrified by Strayer. He held his three-hour weekly seminars in his office, a couple of hundred yards from the Firestone Library. Before the seminar met I would often go into the washroom inside the entrance to Firestone and throw up. Strayer assumed we already knew history; his job, he thought, was to make us into research technicians. All student reports were to be based on original sources although he expected us to master the modern scholarly literature on our own, even though he provided no bibliography. His attitude was: "show me you are a scholar or leave. My way or the highway." He did not turn on the lights in his narrow, gloomy office during his seminar so that students would give their reports extemporaneously and not read their notes; he considered the latter abominably unacademic.

He was at that time a heavy smoker. After two or three cigars, Joe would solicit a couple of cigarettes from the students and finish off with one or two pipefuls of cheap pipe tobacco. He finished the horrible three hours by rubbing his pipe against his cheek in impatience and complaining that we were not good enough researchers. His method was to push us until we broke.

Strayer once assigned me the task of finding, from original documents, of course, how St. Louis IX raised the money for his expensive thirteenth-century crusade into Egypt. I worked night and day for three weeks, forsaking the spring vacation. "Well, Cantor," he said, "how many documents on this subject did you find?"

"Five."

"No, there are seven," he said. I was crushed. It turned out that one document was unpublished and was in a French archive where Strayer alone had found it. The other was published all right but in a provincial and obscure French journal, long defunct. But it was in the library that I was obviously a failure as a researcher. This is the message he delivered.

Strayer disdained the medieval Church and had nothing but contempt for the papacy, except for its skill in collecting taxes. He would not allow us to discuss intellectual or religious history in his seminar. Only taxation and law which demonstrated "the medieval origin of the modern state," the title of his most widely admired book, were permitted subjects.

One day in my second year with Strayer I rashly proposed to do a report on Thomas Aquinas's theory of kingship. "Perhaps, Cantor, you should transfer to the Philosophy Department. You see, anyone can make sense out of Aquinas. That's easy stuff. But only trained research historians can take on the hard task of analyzing medieval government and law. If we don't do it, nobody will." The point was well-taken, except that perhaps the historian, with his contextual knowledge of politics and law, might be able to see something in Aquinas that the philosophers today couldn't. Of course, I didn't dare say that to Strayer.

In spite of Strayer's tough-minded extreme empiricism and anti-romanticism in his seminar, I saw a different and unexpected side to him when as his teaching assistant for five years (1955–60), I attended all his undergraduate lectures on the High Middle Ages and on English common law and constitutional history. He was no showman but he was an exceptionally fine teacher, clear, well organized, with a knack for explaining the most difficult institutions or pattern of events succinctly and simply. He avoided not burdening the young gentlemen by throwing a ream of medieval names at them. In fact, he went to great lengths to avoid proper names: "the pope," "the king," "a prominent lawyer," "the great lords" were what the students heard from him. If he used a name, he gave at least half a lecture on him.

And it was a him. Except for two or three royal queens, he ignored medieval women entirely. But he knew about the women. He knew about everything in the Middle Ages. He would startle me by suddenly giving a brilliant lecture on medieval science, which he never mentioned in his seminars—and, yes, also on St. Thomas Aquinas. He used notes but lectured mostly extemporaneously in a loud voice and simple and quietly jocular conversational style. He was the most intellectually powerful American or European historian and one of the best writers ever to address himself to medieval political history.

Strayer was a liberal Democrat who held the 1950s Republican governments in quiet contempt. He voted twice for Adlai Stevenson. His closest friend on the Princeton faculty was the New Deal economist J. Douglas Brown, one of the principal authors during the mid-thirties of the Social Security Act. Brown served with dignity, sensitivity, and popularity as Dean of the Faculty. He skillfully managed Princeton's maturation into an eminent university. He always dressed in a black suit and a white shirt. He looked like an undertaker, appropriate for being a great expert on old age pensions.

From observing him for eight years, I concluded that Strayer himself owned exactly three sport jackets and two suits. He always wore loafers. I never saw him without a tie, even when he was playing poker, except at the annual departmental softball game.

In spite of Strayer's contempt for the Republicans, he loyally served the Eisenhower administration as a senior consultant to the CIA, a post to which he was recruited by Princeton alumnus Allen Dulles. In the 1950s, Strayer spent each summer in Washington. During the school year whenever there was a crisis somewhere abroad, I could expect a phone call from Strayer at 10:00 P.M. at my home. "Norman, I have been called to Washington. Please take my lecture tomorrow morning." Then he gave me the subject; often I had to stay up most of the night preparing it.

Fortunately the Firestone Library was open until midnight so I could dash over there and collect the books I needed. When Strayer returned on Monday from Washington, he would summon me to his office and make me repeat the lecture to him word for word. Then he would ask some students in the class what they thought of my lecture. Sometimes he would summon me back to his office a couple of days later and tell me what was wrong about the lecture I had given in his absence.

I once had the temerity to ask Strayer why Allen Dulles thought the CIA needed the advice of a medievalist. His response was different from what I expected. This was not Haskins mucking up the Balkans. "Because medievalists are rational people who make judgments from limited evidence and that is also what the CIA does."

In spite of his liberal proclivities, Strayer had no doubt about the righteousness and wisdom of the Cold War. He believed that in time all dictatorships whether of left or right run down and fall apart from within; people just get tired of all the stress and force needed to maintain an authoritarian regime. In his classes he would frequently ruminate on this theme and predict the demise of the Soviet regime, as indeed happened.

In the eight years I was in frequent contact with Strayer, three as a student, five as his junior colleague, he never invited me to have so much as a cup of coffee with him. Yet he took note of what I was doing and helped me in a paternal way. Told by Mommsen in the summer of 1953 that I was having fiscal problems, Strayer immediately arranged for me to be given a make-work job researching bibliography for the Firestone Library.

Strayer's family life was not a happy one. His wife Lois had done doctoral work in psychology at Harvard, an extraordinary achievement for a woman back around 1930. Yet she never worked at a job. She stayed home, raised two children, and became an overweight alcoholic. Their marriage was a very long and rocky one.

Once a year Strayer invited all the faculty to an evening reception at his home, a 1920s pile he rented cheaply from the university. The furniture was shabby and the pictures are what you buy at Wal-Mart. Plenty of liquor was offered, but there was almost no food. After a couple of hours of uneasy calm, Joe and Lois were likely to get into a shouting match. The faculty cringed and slunk off into the night. It was a scene right out of John O'Hara (who lived in Princeton—I chatted with him many times) or Edward Albee.

Strayer had two children: a daughter and a son. The daughter developed normally. She graduated from Smith, married a Philadelphia lawyer, and gave Joe and Lois grandchildren. The son became the dark cloud over Joe's life and probably a main source of his quarreling with Lois. Strayer's son never finished high school. The only thing he was interested in was driving motorcycles and repairing cars. He ended up living as a garage mechanic in Ohio. He married an obese woman from an evangelical sect. Jerry Blum told me that his son was what made Joe so gloomy and bitter. After Lois died in the early 1980s, Joe suddenly remarried—to Sylvia Thrupp, a steely Canadian medieval historian teaching at Ann Arbor.

A strange thing happened at Joe's memorial service. It was a high Episcopalian service held in the Gothic Princeton chapel, obviously directed by the second Mrs. Strayer. I attended and was shocked. Joe Strayer was no Christian believer, let alone a high Episcopalian. He was a skeptic, perhaps an atheist. He detested all organized religion, especially of the Catholic kind. The main eulogy at Strayer's bizarre memorial service was delivered by Harvard's Thomas Bisson, one of Strayer's students who was a year behind me in graduate school. When I knew Bisson back then he seemed more remarkable for his deep Quaker piety than his scholarship. Yet at Berkeley for twenty years Bisson churned out learned tomes on French coinage and Aragonese feudalism. His eulogy was strictly boilerplate. Going along with the Episcopalian service and the Gothic ambience, Strayer was being memorialized as one of those medieval bishops he detested. Sylvia Thrupp was presumably happy about this farce.

Strayer belonged to the great American generation of the 1940s and 1950s who took America to world power and unprecedented prosperity and also transformed the country's leading universities into the world's greatest centers of learning and research. We shall not see the likes of these giants again, certainly not on university campuses—hard-working, ambitious but in no way corrupt; patriotic; determined to carry out their high ideals and achieve their complex goals; very conscious of training a superior intellectual progeny to succeed them; liberal and humanitarian, but essentially moderate and careful and closely in touch with the singular American past.

I was privileged to be part of this unique time and place and was especially lucky to be a friend of Ted Mommsen, along with Carleton Stanley, the greatest influence in my life.

Theodor E. Mommsen was in many ways different from Strayer, who had hired him precisely for that reason in 1948 from Groton School where he had been vegetating since 1940, two years after he came to the United States. Mommsen covered all the aspects of the Middle Ages that Strayer had no interest in or actively disliked— the Early Middle Ages, the culture of the Catholic Church, the German Empire, art and music. It seemed a very good idea at the time, this complementary match, and it was always very good for graduate students, especially because Mommsen was not only the reverse of Strayer academically but also personally. Mommsen was warm, sympathetic, and outgoing toward students whereas Strayer was cold, aloof, and sometimes cruel.

The problem was that Mommsen disappointed Strayer deeply by failing to produce the big book on medieval historical thought on which he had written some unusually perceptive academic journal articles as preparation. But the big book never appeared and that is why in 1954, when Mommsen got "the call," as he termed it in the German manner, from Cornell to be senior medievalist—an unusually enterprising appointment on Cornell's part engineered by a famous German authority on medieval Latin already on the Ithaca faculty, Max Laistner—Mommsen was still resentfully chafing as an associate professor at Princeton. Of course, Strayer matched the Cornell offer but Mommsen's Prussian pride had been hurt by Strayer, who had stopped talking to Ted from one year to the next, and Mommsen promptly headed for Cornell.

The remote and cold place was a bad environment for him. With the exception of the rising star in U.S. history, David Brion Davis, he thought all his new colleagues were "farmers." The departmental chair was indeed an expert on American agricultural history. Mommsen did attract one brilliant graduate student at Cornell, Karl Morrison, but he found most of his graduate students were women. He had never taught their gender before and they appeared to him to be quirky amateurs and dilettantes.

In 1958–59 Ted was slated to be a visiting professor first at Ohio State, where he would deliver his long anticipated book on medieval historical thought as a series of public lectures, and then in Germany. In July of 1958 he committed suicide with sleeping pills. I have no idea whether the big book would ever have been finished.

Mommsen was six feet tall but he seemed shorter because he walked slouched over. He had the squared-off, typically Prussian head but his temperament was more that of the Bavarian south than the cold and heartless north of Germany. Thomas Mann's *Buddenbrooks* effectively captured the primary tension in Ted's life, the conflict between the German north and south. Ted was almost blind without his glasses. He wore good clothes in a sloppy manner and never seemed to get his tie knotted right.

Mommsen's writer's block had psychological, linguistic, and intellectual roots. He was always overawed by carrying the same name as his illustrious ancestor, the greatest of classicists, whose frightening larger-than-life portrait looked down upon Ted in every house or apartment he occupied. Any therapist would have told him to burn old Mommsen's portrait.

In Weimar Germany Ted Mommsen had no strong ambition to be a scholar. His family pushed him into it. What he would have been happy doing was working as a music and art critic for an upscale newspaper but probably he did not write well and fast enough even in German to be a journalist. For no particular reason his family shipped him off to Vienna to be trained as an East Asian scholar by a cousin who was a master of the field. Ted could not learn the languages and returned to Berlin two years later in ignominy. He took a quick Ph.D. in medieval history at Berlin with the senior medievalist, Albert Brackmann.

This was another mistake; Brackmann was already prone to Nazi ideas and in the 1930s became, along with Martin Heidegger, the biggest Nazi academic. Some of this rightist doctrine crept into Ted's doctoral thesis, which upon publication was excoriated in an academic journal by Marc Bloch, the French leftist medievalist. Seeing no opportunity for a teaching job, Ted became a researcher for the German medieval historical institute, *Monumenta Germaniae Historica*. It had a branch in Florence where he was sent to research German-Italian relations in the early fourteenth century.

Mommsen's additional problem that inhibited his writing the big book was that he always had trouble with the English language. He spoke in a heavy German accent, barely comprehensible to under-graduates, and he had even more trouble writing English prose. One of his important articles, published in 1953, I rewrote for him at his request to improve its prose.

Third, Mommsen was beset by the problem that increasingly affected the humanist old culture historians in the 1950s and later. His predilection was toward a highly interpretive kind of history, in effect, historical sociology. He was the nephew of the famous Marianne

Weber, the wife of Max Weber, the greatest of all historical sociologists who died in 1920 (something Mommsen never mentioned until I had known him for three years) and he really wanted to do the kind of historical sociology that Max Weber had done. But Weber's historical conceptualization and recognition of the behavioral sciences was very far from Mommsen's traditional humanist training—Ted never figured out how to do it at all, at least in a big book.

At both Princeton and Cornell in the 1950s, historical sociology seemed outside the parameters of the old British humanist culture, and it was frowned upon among American History Departments. Weberian interpretive history only had some purchase at Columbia. Strayer wrote interpretive history but of a more traditional inductive kind, without the structure and terminology that Weber imposed upon it. Mommsen did not have the courage and self-confidence to break out on his own.

Yet he was dissatisfied and did not want simply to replicate empirical humanist history—narrative based on close documentary analysis. Ted was a man of deep culture and warm temperament and did not fit into the American academic scene of the 1950s. He was similar to Nabakov's *Pnin*. He died too soon. By the late 1960s he would have felt more at home intellectually, although not at Cornell or even Princeton. David Brion Davis had to move on to Yale.

Mommsen became, three weeks into my first seminar with him, my mentor. He not only involved me in the great Romantic traditions of German medievalism going back to the 1880s, but he also introduced me to the complex culture of the medieval Church. He gave me personal advice on how to dress, speak, and behave. He took me to Manhattan on Sunday afternoons to attend concerts of the New York Philharmonic conducted by Bruno Walter. He gave me lessons on wine vintages. He invited me to the house in Princeton that he shared with another bachelor professor, a Renaissance art historian, and endlessly played and critiqued Mozart records for me while he sat in an armchair and stroked his dachshund, Duffer.

After he died, an Ithaca lawyer probating his modest estate informed me that Mommsen in his will had left me the bulk of his library—some three thousand volumes. I kept these books together until 1998, although they were of little use to me, when, feeling old, I gave them away to my graduate students.

I do not know why Mommsen was so good to me. He claimed that I was the genius protégé he had always been looking for to whom he could hand on the torch of Theodor the Elder, his grandfather, and Max Weber, his uncle. I was flattered but I didn't believe him then or now. Perhaps it was a homoerotic attraction to me, but most likely his fabulous generosity to me was the result of guilt feelings about the Holocaust and the Nazis.

If Mommsen had stayed in Germany during the Hitler era, he could have been a powerful Nazi academic. There was not only his patrician lineage to recommend him to the Nazis but also his immediate family—one brother was an admiral during the War; another a big corporation executive first under the Nazis and then in the German Federal Republic. But Ted could not stomach the Nazis. He was not only a liberal but also a philo-Semite. He believed that much of the good things in German culture were Jewish or part Jewish products. Writing medieval history in Germany, the best of it, was heavily a Jewish creation in his view. That two of the greatest names in German medieval scholarship, Ernst Sackur and Erich Caspar, were Jewish and half-Jewish respectively, meant a great deal to him. He worshipped another Jew, Ernst Kantorowicz.

Ted initially kept out of Hitler's way by working in Italian archives for the Berlin Institute. When the job ended in 1938 he headed for the United States. Because faculties were starting to be frozen or reduced in anticipation of the coming war, a position at Yale lasted for only two years. He was rescued from unemployment by being offered a Latin teacher's position at posh Groton School. He admitted to me that he never enjoyed teaching Latin or even on his own, reading the language. He considered it, as I do, a very difficult language and could read it only by close scrutiny and use of a dictionary, not by sight translation.

What Mommsen could have enjoyed in life was reading German literature, attending classical music concerts conducted by German directors, visiting art galleries and archaeological sites in Europe, and dining in good restaurants. Just when this kind of life became possible for him, he killed himself. Some of his friends whispered that he was dying of cancer or grieving for a German woman, the wife of a Johns Hopkins professor who had recently died of cancer herself. Possibly Ted was in a homoerotic relationship with Ernst Kantorowicz and it ended bitterly.

I blame Mommsen's early death on the gloomy and icy ambience of Cornell, symbolizing those deep and primordial gorges there unchanged since the Ice Age covered North America, and on those farmer/professors in the History Department. See Ithaca and die!

Mommsen feared and resented, but still respected, Joe Strayer. For E. Harris (Jinks) Harbison he had only contempt. Harbison's field was what was called in those days "Renaissance and Reformation" (approximately 1350 to 1648). Harbison's original field of research—he published one impressive prize-winning monograph in it as well as a surprisingly dry little survey of the Reformation—was the sixteenth century in England but Jinks insisted on teaching the late medieval Renaissance period, about which Mommsen knew much more. It was not only this common academic rivalry about dividing up teaching fields that tainted their relationship; Mommsen detested what Harbison stood for—what was called White Shoe Presbyterianism.

Harbison and his vivacious wife Jan both came from affluent old Presbyterian families. Harbison was an elder in the Presbyterian Church and was close to many rich and influential Princeton alumni, of which he was one. Harbison's tall thin frame and sharp features were common among rich Princeton alumni. I still see such people in the Princeton Club of New York.

It was constantly bruited about in 1958 that Harbison was on the short list to be chosen the new president of Princeton. But he had to stand down from the competition to fill the upcoming vacancy because he discovered that he had emphysema from chain smoking cigarettes. He died prematurely and painfully of this lung disease in the early 1960s.

Harbison had a very happy marriage and doted on his son John whom he frequently said would become an important classical composer. This turned out to be true. Harbison *fils* is professor of musicology and a celebrated modernist composer at Harvard.

Jinks was too busy in church and academic politics to keep up with all the current historical literature in his field and he did not enjoy reading German. But in terms of sheer mental power, he was pre-eminent among my teachers. I have never met a historian with his native ability for high level conceptualization in cultural history.

In my fourth semester at Princeton, I found myself in a seminar group of one, alone facing Harbison week after week on the Renaissance and early Reformation. Each week he would assign me a report based on six to ten books. I would read them and come back with a thirty-minute oral report that he usually would tear to shreds, pointing out in biting terms how slovenly my thinking was.

Facing Strayer was like facing heavy artillery; Harbison was more like an incoming heat-seeking missile, whistling in on my vulnerabilities, especially my mawkish romanticism. Jinks was a fanatical Calvinist. Leaning back in his office chair—smoking through a filtered cigarette holder which was no use at all in protecting his health—he would bring down the wrath of God upon my intellectual sins. He was an immensely popular undergraduate teacher by the sheer force of his charismatic intellect. I have no doubt that he would have been a great university president and national educational leader. Instead Princeton got in 1958 a young lackadaisical classicist as president who had just been turned down by his own department for tenure—Robert F. Goheen.

That Harbison, for once disagreeing with his friend Strayer's judgment, took the lead in blocking my tenure at Princeton was no surprise to me. He looked upon me as clever and facile, but unpredictable, impetuous, and untrustworthy, not a white shoe Princeton type. He was not wrong. What did surprise me was that his dislike for me by the spring of 1960 was so intense that when he heard that Columbia had offered me tenure, he phoned the Renaissance historian at Columbia, Garret Mattingly of Spanish Armada fame, and urged Mattingly to intervene and get the offer to me canceled. Mattingly told Harbison to go to hell. It seems likely that Harbison could not forever repress a vestigial anti-Semitism.

A couple of years after I began teaching at Columbia, Mattingly came to my office one day and said he was departing for Oxford and because his health was bad, he might not make it back across the

Atlantic. He made me promise that I would supervise his thesis-writing doctoral students until his successor in Renaissance history was appointed. Mattingly died in Oxford. So for two years I carried the burden of supervising dissertations on sixteenth- and seventeenth-century Catholics, a subject about which I knew nothing until that point. But I owed a great debt to Mattingly for his rebuffing of Harbison in 1960.

Mommsen thought my studying with the White Shoe Calvinist Harbison was a waste of time. Instead he wanted me to work with the master of medieval art history, Kurt Weitzmann. As I was preparing to register for my second semester, Mommsen announced that art history would be my minor field outside the History Department and sent me to McCormick Hall, the ornate art history building that housed the precious Index of Christian Art, the world's largest depository of photographs of medieval art, to get admitted to Weitzmann's seminar.

I found him in a duplex office and research center that had been especially built for him and that he generously shared with the few graduate students who met his very high standards. Weitzmann was a disciple of the founder of art history, Aby Warburg, and Warburg's prime disciple, Erwin Panofsky. Panofsky, having created both the Princeton Art History Department and the NYU Institute of Fine Arts, now resided across town at the Institute for Advanced Study.

Weitzmann was a tall, heavyset man who wore only dark suits in winter and seersucker suits in summer. He looked like a German-Jewish banker. Weitzmann left Berlin for Princeton in 1936 and stayed there for the rest of his career. He died at an old age in 1995 after living in retirement in the German-speaking part of Switzerland.

Weitzmann had no small talk. He always came right to the point as he did now when I appeared at his office. He accepted me into his seminar because Mommsen had told him I had proved myself by the exalted standards of German scholarship. Then he asked how many undergraduate courses in art history I had taken. I replied none, because the Canadian college I went to had no Art History Department. The college couldn't afford one and besides the Protestants who ran the place thought pretty pictures were sin. Instead of scornfully telling me to go away, Weitzmann simply suggested that I attend his lectures in his undergraduate medieval survey course while I also attended his seminar. By the end of the semester it would all come together, he said.

It did indeed, to such an extent that Weitzmann, after I had delivered my term paper orally to the seminar, called me in for a private chat and said I should transfer to the art history department and become his student. I thought about this for two weeks and then demurred: I knew a lot of history but still only a bit of art history; I would lose a year or two while I retooled. Additionally, I knew not a word of Greek, an essential language in the field. Thirdly, I told Weitzmann I was badly color-blind and could not distinguish between red, orange, and green. "That doesn't matter," he said, "We are not doing aesthetic criticism. We are studying the ideas in the pictures and where they came from."

I could see myself in the midst of the perpetual conflict then going on (and still today) between the disciples of Warburg—Panofsky and Weitzmann—who pursued the method of iconology (relating picture to the text that allegedly determined the contents of the picture) and those like Meyer Schapiro at Columbia who followed a more sociological approach to medieval art.

Indeed Schapiro was one of Weitzmann's bêtes noires. Meyer Schapiro's name was never to be mentioned in Kurt's seminar. The other no-no was drinking Coca-Cola during the fifteen-minute seminar break in the Chancellor Green cafeteria. Coca-Cola stood for U.S. materialism and mass culture. Coffee, preferably black, was what real humanists drank, Weitzmann declared. I complied, just as I complied with his iconological method.

Weitzmann was a formalist. Once the form (pattern, motif) or iconology of a particular theme had been established—in late antiquity—it would be endlessly copied in all of Christendom, East and West, with only the smallest variation. Schapiro was a social constructivist. In his study of twelfth-century Romanesque art, he tried to find the cultural and social contexts from which the forms or iconology of that style emerged. Schapiro had theoretically the better of the argument but he lacked the erudition to effect a convincing thesis; his main interest lay actually in twentieth-century modernist art. Medieval art was only a sideshow for him to gain respectability and tenure at Columbia.

I was always amused by the contradiction that lay at the bottom of my venture into art history. I was a student of Weitzmann the formalist. But my innate proclivity lay with Schapiro the social constructivist.

The differences between Weitzmann and Schapiro were not as great as seemed on the surface. If Schapiro had been brought up in Germany, he would likely have become a formalist. If Weitzmann had been educated in New York, he would likely have turned into a social constructivist. The greatest name in the 1950s medieval art history, Erwin Panofsky, who was in fact Weitzmann's mentor, saving him from the Nazis, flitted uneasily between formalism and constructivism.

The other two students in the seminar from the art history department bristled at the Weitzmann method and constantly bickered with him. I was too dumb and unsophisticated about art to do so. I rigidly adhered to his method and was hailed by Kurt as a genius. When I came to the first meeting of the seminar Weitzmann had not yet appeared, so I asked the two students "is this considered a difficult course?" "It must be," one of the students replied, "we both flunked last year." And they flunked again, fighting formalist iconology to the bitter end.

Weitzmann's method was relatively simple to understand and resembled the formalist method of interpreting the history of medieval literature propounded by Ernst Robert Curtius (1948), then the rage and still important. Weitzmann insisted that the prototypes of medieval art subjects, how something was depicted, had all been developed in late antiquity and the Patristic era (250–650). The prototype pictures were originally meant to illustrate particular written texts. Often in later medieval centuries, text and picture became dissociated and the picture might end up accompanying a different text. The task of the art historian was to rebuild the cultural tradition by going back and finding the original text that had shaped the contents of the illumination. Rigidly applying this method was for me relatively easy to do. It constituted a paper chase through the texts, nearly always ecclesiastical, of late antiquity and the Patristic era, to find the original text.

The question is: Is this formalistic approach of the German school of art history historically valid? That remains the controversial issue but the iconological, formalistic, picture-to-text German method remains dominant in the study of the art of the medieval and early modern period (before 1750) in the two great Anglophone schools of art history, the Warburg Institute in London and the Institute of Fine Arts of New York University.

Modern art is a different matter. For the modern era Marxist and feminist social constructivists, placing art in the context of social change has become dominant. Weitzmann, who began each day at 9:30 A.M. in his office by reading the *New York Times* for thirty minutes and cursing at the follies of American materialism and cold warriors, would have been distressed at this retreat from iconology.

Weitzmann was just the opposite of Harbison. The latter's learning was clearly limited but he had massive intellect and capability of conceptualization. Weitzmann's intellectual capacity was more limited but his learning was prodigious and his devotion to research boundless. He had absolute mastery of all published pictures and a great many unpublished from the Middle Ages. No computer can return as much data as Kurt could and relate the pictures all to each other and to literary texts, and so quickly and thoroughly.

Weitzmann was a master of the mainline humanistic tradition of texts and cognate pictures. He refused to recognize that the behavioral and social sciences and psychology had something to contribute to understanding art.

To store up artistic material and retrieve it so elegantly required infinite labor, especially in the pre-computer era. It was no task for dilettantes. Sharing his office with Weitzmann, I determined to discover when after midnight he actually left to go home to his art historian wife in a shabby apartment above a restaurant on Nassau Street. At 2:00 A.M. he was still working on his Byzantine illuminations, with the help of coffee, but not Coca-Cola. I gave up and went to bed. At 9:30 A.M. he appeared at his office fresh and well-groomed, ready to peruse the *New York Times* before getting back to work.

The high point of Weitzmann's long and illustrious career involved his study of the early medieval illuminated manuscripts at the monastery of St. Catherine in the Sinai Desert. Here far from imperial-centered power in Constantinople there had survived many illustrated manuscripts that had been executed in the early centuries before the so-called iconoclastic controversy of the eighth century. At that point imperial directives sought the elimination of all religious images partly because the monasteries that housed these icons had gained political power through the population's adoration of icons held by the monks; and possibly also as an effort by a new imperial dynasty from Anatolia—eastern Turkey—to appease Muslim and Jewish populations in that religious borderland.

Hundreds of thousands of religious images—sculptures, mosaics, illuminated manuscripts—were destroyed before the imperial throne again came into the hands of the iconodules (image-lovers) rather than the iconoclasts (image-breakers). The greater part of the artistic heritage of late antiquity in the Greek Church was destroyed. Today this vast body of artwork would be valued at tens of billions of dollars.

The old manuscripts at St. Catherine's in the Sinai were revealed by Weitzmann to provide access to this earlier art before the iconoclastic era. He got permission from the monks to photograph the illuminations, many hundreds of them. Taking these black and white photos back to his research office in Princeton, Weitzmann related the pictures to classical and patristic texts and recreated many themes and prototypes in early Byzantine art that would otherwise have been lost to us forever.

This was one of the great archaeological stories of the twentieth century and it is yet unknown to the public at large. It represents the high point of the old academic culture—selfless, laborious, immensely learned, empirical. Weitzmann did not ruminate on the lost art of early Byzantium; he recreated it for us in significant measure. There was no behavioral theory involved, no sociology or anthropology. His work was the application of empirical reason and infinite learning to articulate a vast artistic culture.

❖ ❖ ❖

Ernst Kantorowicz was also engaged in recreation and discovery —of the ceremony and ideology of medieval kingship and where its roots lay in the Mediterranean and European past before the High Middle Ages of the thirteenth century. But there was a political and cultural purpose to Kantorowicz's work. He aimed to go beyond restoration to inspiration, to recreate the cultural forms of the medieval world for use in the current politics of culture of Weimar Germany in the 1920s. This makes academic consciousness at once more immediately meaningful and socially relevant and yet makes the academic humanities more vulnerable to criticism because of their services to present-day partisanship.

From his undergraduate lectures that I attended in the spring of 1952, it was readily apparent that Weitzmann knew that the Middle Ages could be absorbed into partisan positions in twentieth-century political and cultural wars. But in his many important books, he avoided going down that controversial road. Kantorowicz was actually recruited into medieval studies by the political and cultural ideology of the early twentieth century.

From the other end of verdant Tigertown in the fall of 1951 loomed the mystical figure of Ernst Hartwig Kantorowicz who arrived in Princeton from Berkeley about the same time as I got there from Canada. EKA, as he was called, had been fired from his tenured position at Berkeley in 1950 for refusing to take a state-mandated anti-Communist loyalty oath. He said that as a member of the Free Corps, a proto-Nazi group of demobilized army and naval officers, he had shot Communists in the streets of Berlin in 1919. That proved, he claimed, that he was no Communist, but the California Governor's office was unmoved; no oath, no job.

EKA immediately got an appointment at the Institute in Princeton. Robert Oppenheimer, father of the atom bomb and the Institute director, was a colleague of EKA's at Berkeley in the early 1940s and the head of the Humanities faculty at the Institute was his friend Erwin Panofsky.

EKA, who never lacked for money, bought a handsome house two doors down from Albert Einstein's and moved in his magnificent library and worked mostly at home on the English version of his book on medieval political thought, which was titled *The King's Two Bodies* (1957), still a much studied and debated work. The book which made EKA celebrated in Weimar Germany, however, was a neo-romantic biography of the thirteenth-century German-Sicilian emperor Frederick II. The 500-page book, passionately written in the ornate style of late German romantics, full of all sorts of arcane knowledge, ended with an encomium for the return of a Great Leader in Germany. Appropriately on the book's cover there was a swastika, which by 1928, when the book was first published in German, had been taken by the Nazis as their special emblem.

The Nazi leadership loved the book, which became a best-seller. EKA was catapulted from academic obscurity to the chair of medieval history at the University of Frankfurt. Actually, Kantorowicz had gotten his Ph.D. in Chinese economic history and had undertaken the Frederick II biography at the behest of his mentor, the poet and cultural theorist Stefan George who propounded a kind of mystical fascism.

Kantorowicz came from a very wealthy Prussian-Jewish family. They were the Bronfmans of Weimar Germany, very big in the liquor business. EKA grew up with the descendants of the old Prussian aristocracy. In the Great War he was an army captain posted to Istanbul to show the Turks how to stop the British invasion of Gallipoli, which they did. EKA was an aesthete, an art collector, a connoisseur of fine clothes and vintage wines, and very gay, as were all members of the circle of Stefan George.

At Berkeley during the late 1940s, EKA put together a circle of adoring students, which was not, however, exclusively gay and even included one woman and a heterosexual undergraduate from Winnipeg, Alan Gotlieb, later Canada's ambassador to Washington. EKA's "favorite" was "Bobchen," Robert L. Benson, whom EKA transformed from a Los Angeles beach bum into a medieval history graduate student and brought with him to finish his doctorate at Princeton.

Joe Strayer held EKA in contempt as a scholar and detested him as a man. Strayer regarded EKA as decadent Eurotrash out of whose rotten soil Nazism had sprouted. Strayer barely tolerated Benson. When Benson gave a report in his seminar Strayer always sat poker-faced and made no comment.

Benson's character is shown by the following incident. In the fifth week of Mommsen's seminar in the fall of 1951, Bill Bowsky and I had been slaving for two whole days on our combined translation of the thirty pages of tough ecclesiastical Latin Mommsen had assigned for the week. Benson burst in on us in our carrel and said that he had not been able to do the translations because he had spent the week sparring with his trailer-trash wife and could he just this once borrow our work. Reluctantly we agreed and turned over our precious text for Benson to copy out. When the seminar began, Benson immediately began exhibiting the translations as his own, impressing Mommsen. We never let Bobchen near our work again.

Mommsen, who had known EKA in Germany, worshipped him not only as a great historian, but also as a cultural force. Beyond a doubt Ted adored EKA and EKA in return wrote highly emotional letters to Ted. Whether there was physical sex between them, I do not know.

It is also possible that EKA was bisexual. One sunny day in 1952 while I was walking with Mommsen on Fifth Avenue and heading for Carnegie Hall, Mommsen was suddenly stopped on the street and embraced by a heavily made-up, well-dressed blonde who was, as they said in those days, "stacked." Ted introduced me, they exchanged pleasantries and after the blonde (a 1950s mistress from Central Casting) had moved on, Ted explained to me that this was EKA's "friend." He saw the astonished look on my face and laughed and said nothing further. EKA was indeed either bisexual—playing the gay in Princeton and something quite different in Manhattan—or more likely the brassy blonde was what was then called a "beard," a woman used to disguise gay behavior. Why EKA would have had to engage in sexual pretense at the sophisticated European-dominated Institute is unclear.

The anti-Semitic exclusionary Nuremberg laws of 1935 deprived EKA of his professorship but the Nazi government under the aegis of EKA's friend, Reichmarschall Hermann Goering, continued to pay his salary. So he settled down, with his splendid art collection, in a comfortable Berlin apartment. In 1938 EKA's British gay friend, the classical scholar, poet, and Oxford don Maurice Bowra, visited EKA in Berlin and warned him of the imminence of war in which all Jews would be savaged and told him it was time to leave. EKA abandoned his art collection, packed a bag with his fine clothes, and headed with Bowra for Paris and beyond to London and Oxford.

EKA stayed a year in Oxford where he was hated by the medieval history faculty as phony and ultra-romantic and was offered no job.

Berkeley advertised in the London *Times* for a medievalist who could teach English constitutional and legal history. Although he knew next to nothing about the subject, EKA responded and was given the job. The Berkeley professor who had placed the ad and made the appointment was one of Charles Haskins' ubiquitous brood of students, who became famous in the University for two things: he never published anything and he had the largest classical record collection in the Bay Area. Here was a man who could appreciate EKA.

I had little to do with EKA until the spring of 1957. He did not offer a course at the University but instead at Mommsen's urging he conducted in his house an unofficial seminar, which had been renowned in California, on Dante's *Monarchy*, a prose work of political theory and imperialist propaganda. The seminar met in EKA's handsome living room with its California wicker furniture. Cheap California white wine flowed freely and EKA, urged on by Bobchen Benson, carried on like an egotistical talk show host, reading a line or even a word from Dante and then parading his learning in a half-dozen languages, explicating all possible precedents or relevance to what Dante was saying (which was, in fact, rather simple). I attended for two sessions and gave up, to Mommsen's dismay. I thought that EKA was just showing off. Whatever he was doing in my eyes was not history, and the cheap white wine gave me a headache.

EKA turned up on the defense of my doctoral dissertation at Mommsen's behest and asked some very good questions and besides pointed out some errors in my Latin translations. The day before the exam he phoned me out of the blue and told me about the German tradition of the successful Ph.D. candidate feting his examiners afterwards. I did that with good food and expensive wine that I could ill afford. After an hour of cheering refreshment, I noticed Joe Strayer actually talking to EKA, perhaps for the first and last time. It was a precious Princeton moment.

In the spring of 1957—just before my marriage—EKA discovered that I lived in a third floor apartment in an old house that was just behind his own and on the shortcut for his nightly walk for a German deli, long since gone, on Palmer Square, the elegant heart of downtown Princeton. If he saw a light in my apartment as he walked by, he would call to me from the street and I would join him in his ten-block walk back and forth. This went on for about three months. He always bought exactly the same thing at the deli—two red Delicious apples and a quarter pound of Westphalian ham, presumably his dinner—this was around 8:00 P.M. Frequently on the way back we would stand talking in front of my house for a half hour. After a spell of this he invited me to his home for a drink of that horrible California white wine and we talked at length while he ate his apples and ham.

I now got a chance to examine his library and it was marvelous. It was full of huge seventeenth-century printings of medieval texts. These folio volumes on stout rag paper could be bought after the War for a song. He told me what was wrong with my dissertation and how I should improve it before publication. (I listened gravely but didn't follow his advice.) Then we talked at length about all sorts of medieval subjects, including his great admiration for the English legal historian Frederick William Maitland who died in 1906. I shared his admiration for Maitland but for different reasons than EKA.

I noticed that as the time passed, EKA dropped his customary singsong way of speaking, an affectation of Prussian aristocrats just as stuttering is a mannerism of the English aristocracy. He sounded now and looked like a German-Jewish émigré in Hollywood—producer or director. He could have been Billy Wilder.

By this time the German government had paid EKA extensive reparations for losing his job because of anti-Semitic exclusion and for his abandoned art collection. How much he was compensated for Nazi seizure of his family's liquor empire I do not know. EKA used the money to go to Las Vegas each August and spend a month at the gambling tables.

There he wrote—on a typewriter—sentimental letters to Mommsen in Princeton. Two such letters came into my possession after I inherited Ted's library in 1958. They were inserted in pages of books. Still a Canadian puritan, I foolishly destroyed the letters. It is hard to judge the significance of these seemingly emotional letters. If they were written in the 1950s from one American-born academic to another, it would be probable that a homoerotic relationship existed between them. But upper middle-class and aristocratic Germans of that generation had a propensity to write to each other in highly emotional terms that might reflect current neo-romantic convention rather than private feelings.

EKA's path and mine crossed one final time. Early in 1958 Strayer summoned me to his office and told me that the *American Historical Review* was having a hard time finding a reviewer for EKA's *magnum opus, The King's Two Bodies.* I remember Strayer saying with a rare smile that no fewer than eleven senior medievalists had turned it down presumably because they disliked the book but were afraid to say so in a review because as a senior professor at the Institute, EKA commanded vast patronage in the form of visiting research professorships. Strayer said that for obvious reasons of academic propriety he himself couldn't do it, but maybe I could, as he held out a copy of the book. I wrote the review and it was damning and created a fuss among EKA's coterie of acolytes headed by Bobchen Benson.

I was told that EKA was furious with me; indeed, I never heard from him again. That fruity German poseur had been deflated at last; Strayer was immensely pleased. In retrospect, while the things I said in criticism of EKA's book were true enough, they weren't important compared to the positive things I should have said. Although it was a work that from the point of view of empirical political and legal history was of small consequence, it was an exhibition of the structural cross-currents of medieval high political culture, what nowadays would be termed the medieval discourse. In this regard it was a pioneering work of great value, although oddly constructed and hard to read.

The King's Two Bodies was seminal scholarship in that within the oppressive framework of conventional German history of ideas Kantorowicz was trying to illuminate a structural portrait of the high ecclesiastical culture of the High Middle Ages, as distinctive and sophisticated a culture as has ever existed.

EKA was greatly hampered by his ignoring of the social and behavioral sciences and his self-conscious effort to please the magnates of the Medieval Academy like Strayer, which he could never do. But read today his book anticipates the postmodern deconstructionist kind of medievalist inquiry pursued in the 1990s by Caroline Walker Bynum and Gabrielle Spiegel.

Mommsen had a sense of where EKA was trying to go. Blinded by Strayer in 1958, I did not. Mommsen died a couple of weeks before my shabby review appeared and he never saw it. It would have hurt Ted deeply.

The culture of the Princeton History Department in the late 1950s, as well as other humanities departments in that university, of which Art History, English, and Philosophy were the best, was the highest development ever achieved in the United States by the old academic culture derived from British humanism and spiced up a bit with traces of French and German thought and Italian art. By 1960, much the same level of intellectual and educational productivity was attained at other Ivy League universities, plus the University of Chicago and the University of California at Berkeley. The standards were very high, the quality of faculty unprecedented on this side of the Atlantic, and the achievements in learning and research still appear remarkable.

As with all cultural systems at high level of development, especially after a rapid improvement in quality and visibility, the Princeton humanists thought their discourse would never be challenged. They assumed that the thought-world they had molded was on a straight line involving infinitely further progress. It was not to be. Those sunny times would end shortly and there would be confusion, disappointment, and deterioration. Then in the mid-seventies a new culture would start to emerge in the major American universities to which has been given the name postmodernism.

A weakness of Princeton and the other bastions of the old British-based humanist print culture in the 1950s was that its protagonists had no understanding that a communications and media revolution was underway with television, film, and rock music that would contend against their linear and rationalist text-based mentality. Marshall McLuhan had published his first major book proclaiming that the medium was the message but his name never came up among the Princeton faculty with whom I consorted.

Many Princeton History Department faculty still did not own TV sets and if they did, they said all they could find on it was trash, the detritus of a mean, low, irrational, insensate mass culture they detested. They may have been right from one point of view, but they were deficient in social perception. They could only stand back and look with dread at the new media transmitters and the vulgar software that went with it. They were not in the least populists, whatever their political stripe. They wanted to have nothing to do with the American mass mind. They were poorly prepared for the upheavals of the sixties and seventies.

The high-flying departments like Princeton History slowly got themselves into a squeeze between the aggressive perpetuation of research-driven scholarship on the one side and the obligation to teach well and communicate to the public at large on the other. Princeton administrators talked glibly of hiring and retaining "scholar teachers" so there were no tensions among the three commitments of a first-class History Department.

But by 1960 it was becoming difficult to reconcile the three functions of humanities professors. Under James B. Conant as President of Harvard, a chemist and bureaucrat, scholarly research was made the distinctive criterion for tenure there after the sixth year of teaching, claiming—falsely—that good teaching and public communication would follow naturally along. The other Ivy League universities, those with doctoral programs, like Princeton, could not resist taking the Harvard line, which was also that of the best state university, Berkeley.

I was an early victim of this hard line Conant policy. I published my doctoral dissertation in 1958, a year after taking my degree. It was controversial. It was staunchly praised by one of the three or four best American medievalists, Sidney Painter at Johns Hopkins, and by a prominent church historian in Germany, and severely criticized by a couple of Oxbridge dons. It was good enough to pass muster as a work of significant scholarship and it was also well written. Princeton University Press's too modest print run of one thousand copies of the book sold out within ten months of publication. It was then taken up by another publisher and remained in print until 1994.

I made token gestures to preparation of a scholarly sequel but instead devoted my time to teaching (including a course in modern British history, outside my original field, drawing heavily on what Stewart Reid had taught me at United College) and public communication.

In 1959 I accepted an offer of a contract from New York Macmillan to write a new culturally focused survey of the Middle Ages that could be used not only as a textbook (thereby competing with Strayer's two textbooks in the field), but also be accessible to the educated reader in general. The book appeared in 1963, got a rave review in *The New Yorker*, and was a main selection of the History Book Club.

But Princeton did not wait to see if I could achieve my goal of bringing medieval history to the middle-class lay reader. The majority of the tenured faculty led by Jinks Harbison—but not including Joe Strayer—decided I was not Princeton History material. Not only did I have no private means like half of the departmental faculty, and I couldn't play poker and was socially gauche in general, but I was not going to be the ready producer of conventional research monographs, which under Harvard influence was now their main currency of academic value.

Between January and May of 1960 I got tenured associate professor offers, with a substantial raise in my very modest and unlivable salary, from Johns Hopkins and Columbia. Hopkins wanted me to replace Sidney Painter who died suddenly in January 1960 of a heart attack. I commuted to Baltimore and taught his graduate students in the spring semester of 1960. They hated me, somehow feeling I had caused their beloved master's death.

Columbia wanted me to teach the required course on the history of the common law for eighty pre-law students a semester. This course had been taught by the American aristocrat Robert Livingston Schuyler for thirty years. He retired in 1958 and the instructors tried out in the course during the next two years had bombed. The Department Chair, Richard B. Morris, the son of a Brooklyn rabbi, the first full-blooded Jew aside from the holder of an endowed chair in Jewish history to teach in the Columbia History Department (beginning in 1947), heard about me from his son, who was in my course at Princeton.

Under pressure from the Dean to find a good teacher for the impor-tant course on English legal history, Morris invited me to have lunch with him in the Columbia faculty club on Morningside Drive. An hour later he offered me an untenured associate professorship. I said not only would he have to give me tenure, but he would also have to intervene with the U.S. Immigration Service who on abstruse technical grounds were making it hard for me to get a permanent immigration visa.

The immigration problem arose because of a mistake in the Dean's office at Princeton, who told Strayer they could not rectify their error and I would sooner or later have to go back to unwelcoming, still anti-Semitic Canada for two years before getting a green card. Frederick Lane, the Hopkins Chair, offered me tenure but could not see how to solve my immigration problem.

Richard Morris, a Jew who got things done, said, "Go back to Princeton and start preparing to move to New York. I will get you tenure from the provost and I will get my friend Harry N. Rosenfeld, the best immigration lawyer in the country, to solve your little immigration problem."

I went back to Princeton that April day with my head swimming and was in Strayer's office the next morning. "How much money did Dick Morris offer you?" he said, sucking on his cigar. "Nine thousand," which was $1,500 more than I was getting at Princeton. Without cracking a smile, Strayer remarked: "Those people at Columbia will stop at nothing." He told me he would discuss the matter of tenure with the Department's full professors. A week passed and nothing happened. I sent him a note saying I had to know by tomorrow or I would accept the Columbia offer. I had not told Strayer that Morris had promised to resolve my visa problem, which the Princeton bureaucracy claimed they couldn't do.

The next day passed into late evening without a word from Strayer. Finally at 10:30 P.M. on Thursday—it was poker night at Elmer Beller's and I suppose the call came from there—Jerome Blum called. "Joe wanted me to tell you that the Executive Committee did not reach a decision in your case. You have been here only five years. This would be a premature tenure case. You have another year before your tenure decision has to be made. Joe wants you to turn down Hopkins and Columbia and stay here another year and then we will make a decision," said Jerry with some hesitancy.

"Will Strayer promise me a positive decision on tenure next year?"

"Norman, you know he cannot do that. You need a majority vote of all the full professors."

The next morning at 9:00 A.M. I phoned a delighted Dick Morris and told him I was coming to Morningside Heights and handed Strayer's secretary a letter of resignation effective August 31. Strayer did not speak to me again for ten years and then only after, as editor of a history book series for the Dial Press, I arranged a big advance for him for a book on the Albigensian Crusade—a classic that is still in print.

The day after I accepted Morris's offer, Harry N. Rosenfeld, Deputy Commissioner of Immigration in the Roosevelt Administration, phoned me from New York. Like all big lawyers he preferred to deal with small clients by phone rather than face to face. I explained my situation. He asked me to send him several documents and told me his fee would be $500 (ten times that in 2002 dollars). I asked him what his regular fee was for a case like mine. "At least $5,000."

"How do you know," I asked, "that you can win my case?"

"Your case will go to a three-man review board in Washington in the Justice Department's Immigration Section. When I was Deputy Commissioner I appointed all those three guys; they owe me plenty." Two months later I had my visa approval. Even then it was only a 2–1 vote of the board. One of the members of the board had dared to vote against his benefactor, Harry Rosenfeld.

While I was packing the books in my office early in July and the campus was deserted, Elmer Beller came by, "I am very sorry to see you leave, you are a very good teacher and a good scholar, even if some of my colleagues think otherwise. This is a big loss for us. I am sure in a few years we will invite you back." Of course that didn't happen.

In the mid-1960s after Strayer quit as Chair, control of the Department was taken over by the Oxford Marxist Lawrence Stone. Jerry Blum, for reasons I never learned, engineered this coup. Stone brought in from Berkeley his feminist leftist ally, Natalie Zemon Davis. Together they conducted a twenty-year vendetta against me, telling their graduate students I was a phony and a reactionary.

When Strayer retired from teaching in the late 1970s, he was succeeded by one of his two African American graduate students, William Chester Jordan, who was also very close to Lawrence Stone and who also spoke to his students about me in contemptuous terms. Yet Strayer at one point told Bryce Lyon, the medievalist at Brown University, that I was the best student he ever had—and also the best pitcher on the departmental softball team.

Dick Morris's appointment of me to tenure without a formal review by the tenured faculty was probably irregular. But he got the support of another history professor, Jacques Barzun, who was also the Provost and decided on tenure appointments. Columbia required for promotion or appointment to tenure not only a departmental recommendation but also the recommendation from an ad hoc Committee of five full professors from outside the Department of the nominee.

There was, however, a loophole in this apparently austere system. The ad hoc panel was chosen by the Provost. Among the large Columbia faculty he knew who were the hard-liners and who were the softies. He could, if he wanted, put together a panel that would have caviled at the appointment of Albert Einstein, and one that would approve of any name put before them. I suppose that the panel selected in my case by Jacques Barzun leaned more toward the latter than the former complexion.

Yet I was not an unworthy candidate. I had published a highly visible, if controversial, dissertation and I had an important interpretive article on medieval monasticism coming out that very summer in the *American Historical Review*, which did not publish many medieval articles.

In any case, as far as the Columbia History Department was concerned, support for me by both Dick Morris and Jacques Barzun would have easily gotten me a majority vote of the history faculty for tenure if a formal vote had been held.

Morris ran the department with an iron hand and he was a great historian of colonial America and early American law. Barzun was not only a much admired teacher but also an important historian of modern European culture and a prominent critic. He and his friend in the English Department, Lionel Trilling, were the power brokers in the Columbia humanities departments and Barzun also had the authority of the Provost's office to exercise his choices.

My appointment may not have been entirely conventional but it was justified. In June 1960, at the age of thirty, I received an embossed card from the Secretary of Columbia University, an obscure functionary, informing me that the Trustees had approved my appointment to tenure. It had all the imperial, confident tone of a Governor of India appointing a commissioner in the Punjab.

Nevertheless when I started to move into my office at Columbia that summer, several faculty asked me: "What are you doing here?" I was a bit taken aback to now surmise that Morris had never consulted the whole department; I said I was a tenured associate professor and had been hired to teach the English common law course and medieval intellectual history. There were gasps of astonishment, especially from John Mundy, the senior medievalist, whom Morris held in contempt, although not in as much contempt as he held the professor of ancient history, the phenomenally learned Russian Jew Elias J. Bickerman—"a damned fool in six languages" Morris called him. Mundy, in Morris's eyes, was simply mediocre; he lacked the "national visibility" that a senior Columbia historian should have. I have no doubt that Morris secretly hoped that in time I would displace Mundy as senior medievalist. Certainly Mundy suspected as much.

My courses at the college level at Columbia were immensely popular. Five years later the full professors, even John Mundy, voted my promotion to their level. My first three years (1960–63) at Columbia were intellectually the most creative in my academic career. It was in every way what a great university ought to be. I got a new education in behavioral science from the sociologists and anthropologists.

I should have stayed at Columbia the rest of my professional life. After my first glorious year at Columbia, as the applause in my common law course after my final lecture died, Princeton seemed small, remote, and far away. In the 1980s I used to drive down to Princeton two or three times a month to work in the newly expanded —not very successfully—Firestone Library.

I stood in front of the Library across from the Gothic chapel, the marvelous Romanesque Chancellor Green Building to my right and it could have been the first week of September 1951. The University had greatly multiplied its outlying buildings but the core in front of Firestone remained exactly the same. At lunchtime I went to the Annex Restaurant across Nassau Street from Firestone. I had been there in 1951 and it was cheap. The menu had not changed in thirty-five years. The Annex was still overrun by professors at lunchtime, even though Princeton now had a lavish Faculty Club, which it did not have in the more austere fifties. At the table next to mine, a professor was engrossed in conversation with a young woman, possibly his daughter. I thought that if things had turned out differently, that could be me, talking with my daughter, now a successful bilingual journalist in Miami.

It was one of those very hot Princeton July days. Princeton's elevation is lower than New York City. In the eighteenth century it was a site of a huge malarial swamp. I drove over to the Graduate College, with its imitation Magdalen tower. The tower was smaller than I remembered. It had been de-Demillized. I drove down to the junior faculty housing development on Stanworth Drive, about a mile from the campus. There I had lived from 1957 to 1960 with my wife, and after 1958, my son, today a maple syrup farmer in Vermont. When my wife and I got an apartment there after being on the waiting list for three months, we considered ourselves privileged, even though the rent consumed a third of my monthly after-tax salary. Now Stanworth looked desiccated, rundown, obsolete. So in a sense did the whole university. It had been the proud culmination of the old academic order. But that era had passed.

What historians and commentators have stressed with regard to the causation of changes in academic culture after the mid-1960s was the changed composition of the student body. It was not just much larger in numbers but it included many students ill-prepared both by high school in cognitive training and family-shaped behavioral patterns to absorb readily the conventional text-based liberal arts curriculum and its intellectual challenges. So there was a watering down of standards, introduction of easier courses, grade inflation on a large scale, and new majors that were relatively undemanding.

This indictment had plausible grounds in the large state colleges and even in some smaller private colleges. But in the Ivy League and the other top thirty colleges in the country, the cognitive capacity of the undergraduate has, in my experience, changed only modestly since the 1950s and not always adversely. It is true that by 1980 it was obvious that many of my students did not like to read and the reading assignments were shortened by me and by many other professors. On the other hand, contrary to media myth, I think students today write somewhat better than in 1960. They are probably a little more intellectually alive, even if they do not any longer come to class carrying a copy of the day's *New York Times.*

It was changes in the faculty much more than in the student body that generated a demographic impact on preservation of the old culture and provided a social context for the rise of the new culture. There were now at the end of the century perhaps 10 percent of the faculty who were black and Hispanic minorities. The Hispanics acted no different from the tweedy white males of the 1950s, at least after they were two or three years into their teaching careers.

The new component of African American faculty split down the middle. Half accommodated themselves well to conventional thought and academic behavior. Half of the African Americans were activists and sometimes overt rebels. But their numbers were too small to have a significant impact on the campus and by the 1990s, the proportion of black faculty who were activists and dissidents had sharply diminished.

The big change was the intrusion of large numbers of women into faculty positions in the humanities and soft (outside economics) behavioral sciences after 1970 under the pressure of federal regulations. By 1995, 40 percent of the assistant professors in history were women and their number was rising fast. As the women got tenure in large numbers, they became visible and steadily more prominent among the tenured faculty. They became departmental chairs and deans. The pattern of women's domination of the humanities by the second decade of the new century is evident. History by 2010 will be like nursing, mostly a female profession.

A change in the employment situation for Ph.D.s after 1974 contributed to the sharp increase in the proportion of younger faculty who were women. By 1974 the expansionary demographic tide of the previous decade was leveling out. In many states including California and New York, the state universities also experienced a slow reduction in their budgets for various political reasons and that further reduced the pace of academic hiring to full-time positions.

There have been after all only two short eras of strong demand for new Ph.D.s on U.S. campuses—the mid-1920s and the decade approximately following 1960. By the mid-1970s the job situation on U.S. campuses for new Ph.D.s went back to its normal adverse condition and this was further aggravated by the overexpansion of doctoral programs to sustain the academic research oligarchy who normally only wanted to teach graduate students.

Because of federal affirmative action guidelines and because of the egalitarian disposition of the deans and departmental chairman, women Ph.D.s in a tight job market by 1980 had at least twice the likelihood of getting an entry level tenure-track position as men. By the mid-1980s the word had gotten around on this prejudice against male Ph.D.s and the best of the prospective male Ph.D.s eschewed graduate work and headed for law and business schools.

Thus by the 1980s women Ph.D.s were much more likely to be hired than men coming out of doctoral programs and the quality of female graduate students, at least in the humanities and soft social sciences, was on average significantly higher than among male students.

By 1990 when you went to the annual meeting of the American Historical Association the male doctoral students looking for work seemed shrunken, sallow, and defensive compared to the women. They knew they were an unwanted breed.

As the number of women graduate students sharply increased in the 1960s, by 1970 there was a spousal problem—what to do with the Ph.D. wife of a newly appointed male Ph.D.? She was usually fobbed off on an ill-paid part-time appointment or to a job in a local community college. A quarter of a century later, there was often a spousal appointment problem but the gender preference had been reversed.

It was the woman in the academic couple whom the department now wanted and the shadowy husband who had to be accommodated somehow. Indeed by the later 1990s the significant other of an intensely recruited senior woman academic was often a younger woman. Lesbian relationships became common among women academic humanists—as they had been in the Seven Sisters colleges in the first two decades of the twentieth century when they were called "Boston marriages."

A common sight at academic conferences offering a thriving job market in the 1990s was the husband feeding and diapering the infant who had been brought along while his wife was busy with the coveted job interviews that he lacked.

The new wave of feminist academics of the 1970s and 1980s, following their doctrine that feminine consciousness was cultural rather than biological, argued that the rise of women portended no change in the character of the humanities disciplines. It has not turned out this way.

Women historians are better at concrete and specific research subjects. They shy away from writing broad interpretive works. They rarely write textbooks and if they do, they are seldom successful. Women academic humanists' favorite form of communication is the research article in an academic journal, and the latter by the end of the 1990s was becoming the standard value of academic currency in the humanities, as it had been in the natural sciences for a long time.

Women historians were also inclined to biographical narratives, preferably of ordinary people. This is why women academics took the lead in joining together history and anthropology, which had long given legitimacy to this kind of writing.

The women faculty in the 1970s and 1980s still felt underappreciated and they were certainly often underpaid. As a result, no matter how intensive their training they carried no torches for the old academic culture, which had previously all but excluded them and now seemed rejectionist and defensive toward them. Sexual harassment in the narrow sense of the term of sexual advances was very rare, but sexual harassment newly defined and broadened out as "a hostile work environment"—there was plenty of that.

Under these conditions women professors in the humanities and soft social sciences were open to theories and ideologies that took a critical and adversarial attitude to the campus traditions and academic hierarchies. They were not activists; they took a low profile in campus politics. The new generation of women academics were in the front rank, however, of supporting and disseminating postmodernist teaching and language that was intellectually adversarial toward the old culture and eager to point out its weaknesses and to transcend some of its salient discourse and central traditions and cognitive character.

The feminization of university faculties was a major contributor to the rise of a new academic culture. The era of the woman in American universities had begun, especially in their humanities faculties and this portended profound cultural and intellectual changes, which are still unfolding.

The old academic culture that reached its high point at Princeton in the 1950s was a legacy of the masculine intellectual world of Victorian and Edwardian Britain. Whether the ingredients and format of this old culture were rooted in biology or were entirely the product of centuries of conditioning or were the consequence of nature and nurture acting together is endlessly debatable. The important point is that it was a well integrated historically masculine culture.

The 1970s and 1980s feminists and their radical male mentors and allies in academia might claim that there was nothing systemically biological about the old culture and hence it would not be significantly altered by women intruding into and advancing within academia. This was held to be just a matter of civil liberties, of giving women equal status and representation on university faculties. But because women academics had been largely excluded for decades from the inner circle of twentieth-century male academia, the era of the Woman in academic life could not just signify a legalistic and demographic adjustment. It was bound centrally to affect and contribute to the rise of a new academic culture.

The Marxists who had been almost totally excluded from American university faculties in the three decades before 1960 and who as a result of the frenetic and careless faculty expansion of the sixties and early seventies were now gaining professorships in substantial numbers, perceived this social reality more clearly than the proponents of the old culture. While the male old culture humanists like myself were congratulating themselves on their newly egalitarian acceptance of women in academia, the Marxist New Left rapidly set about forging an alliance with the younger women faculty. This social and political juncture was central to the rise of a new academic culture.

❖ 4 ❖

TROUBLED UNIVERSITIES
AND THE NEW CULTURE

I n the summer of 1999, a review of my 1997 history of English
common law appeared in the establishmentarian academic journal,
Law and History Review. The reviewer was Rutgers University's Donald
R. Kelley, a prolific and immensely learned historian of early modern
European law (A.D. 1500–1800) and for many years the editor of the
prestigious and intellectually conservative *Journal of the History of Ideas*.
Kelley and I had been colleagues for three years in the early 1970s at
Binghamton University, an upstate campus of the State University of
New York. We tolerated each other, but I, as the chairman of the
History Department, was not sorry to see him leave for the University
of Rochester—from which he later migrated to Rutgers—because he
was an indifferent undergraduate teacher, although no doubt a scholarly
superstar in a department not overly subscribed with this stellar quality.

Kelley prefaced his mixed assessment of my new book with a
summary account of my career: "Cantor began his career in the 1950s
as perhaps the brightest star among American medievalists of that
generation—an extraordinarily popular undergraduate teacher as well as

a fine scholar, whose projected trilogy on church-state relations in the eleventh and twelfth centuries never got beyond an impressive first volume... After that Cantor turned his hand, prolifically... to works of popularization concerning the meaning of the Middle Ages and, off-handedly, the fads and foibles of our own multiculturally embattled times."

There is substance to this censorious evaluation. I did not fulfill my promise as a scholar in the traditional sense. I went down a different road as a writer, one that carries small purchase with Donald Kelley and the academic establishment, in spite of my becoming in time the most read university medievalist among the educated public at large. Kelley and I are not disputing the arc of my career; the main difference lies in the value system through which it is perceived.

Kelley assumes that there are only two kinds of historical writing: (a) research monographs on narrow subjects with lots of footnotes and (b) "popularization." He doesn't allow that the second category, not traditional scholarship, might be broken down into two or more subgroups, one of which is addressing and educating the general public.

From his empyrean position in the academic establishment Kelley also does not allow that personal problems might have affected my career and the kind of writing I came to do.

I never again enjoyed the balanced happiness that I experienced consistently during the 1950s at Princeton—except for the tense denouement in 1960 when I failed to get tenure and had to leave. There was a personal reason for this: I got married and became a parent and tried to support my family on sparse academic salaries. In my first sojourn in New York City from 1960 to 1966 while teaching at Columbia, I never could afford a decent place to live for my family, either in the city or the suburbs. I spent at least an hour each Sunday scrutinizing the *New York Times'* real estate ads. All I learned from this extended exercise was the iron rationality of the market. There were no surprising bargains of good housing that I could afford.

Although my parents continued to take lengthy winter vacations in Miami or Israel, my father claimed that he was constantly on the edge of bankruptcy. The family situation was complicated by my paranoid mother taking extreme dislike for my wife. We had been very close, my mother and I. She had raised me, an only child, while my father was often away at the ranch. Possibly any woman I would have married my mother would have hated. There was bad feeling between my mother and Mindy from the time of our engagement and my mother dissuaded my father from helping us fiscally. My wife's parents were simple, hard-working people of very modest means. My wife had two uncles who were well off but as was customary in Jewish families they were only interested in bettering their children's lot and gave no heed to their niece's needs.

This mean situation had a stringent impact on our marriage; if we had had any money, we would probably have divorced. We stayed together with our two children simply because we were too poor to do otherwise.

This misery affected my capacity to do the kind of slow and close and detailed work that scholarship entails—finishing the trilogy that Kelley mentions. I could write textbooks and narrative history books for the trade or educated public. Indeed, doing this kind of aggressive writing affirmed my humanity in the midst of my domestic problems and humiliating poverty. It also brought me, during the late 1960s after we left New York for Massachusetts, the wherewithal at last to provide a decent environment for my wife and children, and that greatly alleviated the tensions in our marriage.

No matter how distraught I felt creeping home on the filthy subway in New York to bad apartments in north Manhattan or the west Bronx, I could always look forward during the week at any rate to getting back to my campus office early the next morning and, fortified with a rush from sugar donuts and black coffee, resuming my writing. It made me feel calm and free, whereas grubbing around in the university library collecting footnotes made me not only bored and weary, but also imparted a guilty sense that as a primordially conditioned hunter and gatherer I was failing my little family.

Besides this domestic problem there was another that detracted me from a conventional life as the "brightest star among American medievalists." I could not find for long another intellectual home like Princeton in the 1950s. As a student at Oxford and as a professor at Columbia, Brandeis, and Binghamton, there was always something irritating and debilitating or much worse, terrifying and strangulating, to threaten me in the campus ambience. Finally in 1974 I sought a new career as a university administrator that lasted until 1981.

Whenever in the 1980s I drove down to Princeton from Greenwich Village to spend a day in the Firestone Library, the good days of the 1950s haunted me. I saw myself as a denizen of an alternative universe, a lost horizon from which I had been segregated by bad luck and evil people. I saw books on the shelf in the open library stacks that I had read in Mommsen's seminars. I pulled them out and saw my signature on the borrower's card (before computerization wiped all this away). I ran my finger over my old signature and the 1950s date stamp next to it. I pressed my fingers on this articulation of memory. Nothing happened. The alternative universe remained closed to me.

"I am tired to have to devote so much time dealing with your problems," an exasperated Joe Strayer told me in February 1960. I had become a bother, discontent, a troublemaker. The strains of my domestic situation had affected my capacity to act effectively in my professional life. Undoubtedly this played a part. I needed therapy but I had no means to undertake it.

In 1960 I began to read extensively in Freud and this gave me much greater self-knowledge but this was not the equivalent of skillful therapy. In the 1980s and 1990s I finally underwent extensive therapy but it was only with my third therapist, Lynda Zweben-Howland, combined with Prozac and Neurontin, that feelings of anger and extreme depression were significantly alleviated. In the 1950s and 1960s as I found unhappiness in turn at Oxford, Columbia, Brandeis, and Binghamton I did not have the support of therapy. After Mommsen killed himself in the summer of 1958, I lost my primary mentor.

When someone is in conflict with his environment, going angrily from one place to another, prone to rebellion and confrontation, psychological factors rooted at least partly in genetic makeup are in play. But I think my personal and domestic problems only intensified my disappointment and anger with academic institutions. These institutions did have deep flaws. They were in trouble. They chewed people up, including me, and spit them out. Their problems were not random. They were grounded in the conditions of the old culture in its time of maturation. There were now ever-increasing intrinsic defects within the old culture, as well as institutional incapacity to adjust to changing social contexts.

I wanted from the old culture something that it could not give—to apply its material and human resources to the next phase in Western, transatlantic culture. I yearned for an intellectual revolution on campus where the vast humanistic learning that had accumulated since the late nineteenth century would be joined with the concepts of the behavioral and social sciences and thereby would supersede the old culture of the 1950s.

I tried to articulate my feelings and aspirations in an encapsulating term—I called it "comparative history" (too flat), historical sociology (too jargon-ridden), neo-romanticism (better but frightening); eventually it would fall unsatisfactorily under the rubric of postmodernism. It involved synthesis of traditional learning with vanguard ideas from human sciences and attentiveness to contemporary popular culture. There was a new world of ideas to be examined and a new kind of history to be written.

If I could have stayed at Princeton and been a power broker in the History Department, perhaps I could in time have shifted Princeton's resources and prestige toward the new culture. But my teachers and colleagues had cast me out because they saw in me a personal and intellectual restlessness and an insatiable ambition that they could not abide. I hoped in succession that Oxford, then Columbia, then Brandeis, then Binghamton would be the welcoming environment where I could do the work I wanted. But sooner or later there was always something wrong.

I came to Oxford in the fall of 1954 as a Rhodes scholar from Manitoba after three years at Princeton. I had stars in my eyes. I had read that spring, after my selection, every book in the Princeton Library, nonfiction or fiction, that described Oxford in some way. I took to reading British weeklies like the *Times Literary Supplement* and the *New Statesman* to ingratiate myself into British high culture at whose center Oxford (and Cambridge) lay.

I was fixated on the Oxford of 1912 that Carleton Stanley, an Oxford student then, had portrayed for me in the beer hall at United College in 1947. I read with rapture *The Making of the Middle Ages*, a 1953 book by a hitherto obscure Balliol College, Oxford don, Richard W. Southern, that offered a neo-romantic, broadly synthetic, spiritually directed view of the twelfth century. Southern lighted up the horizon of medieval studies in the way that I thought would provide deeper understanding and personal satisfaction and that I identified as the quintessence of Oxford medievalism.

When I arrived at Oxford in September 1954 the old University was in one of its down periods and had not recovered from the War either intellectually or fiscally. Oxford was founded in the second half of the twelfth century so that clerics would not have to pursue what we would call graduate level studies at Paris—and bring back from there dissident ideas that the Crown might not like.

By 1320 the crowded provincial city was home to three thousand students and dons (faculty). In 1954 its student body had reached twelve thousand in a population ten times as big. In 1320, however, there was only one other university in England, the recently established Cambridge (by a group of discontented Oxford faculty and students seceding from Oxford), which was then little better than a cow college in the swamps of East Anglia. Cambridge became a real university in the late sixteenth and seventeenth centuries when it was transformed by activist Protestants as their institution as Oxford became the stronghold of the more conservative Episcopalian tradition.

The more progressive Cambridge was home to Isaac Newton and the Scientific Revolution around 1700, and in the nineteenth and twentieth centuries it was much stronger in the natural sciences and in economics than Oxford. The Cavendish Laboratory in Cambridge was the site of the two most important scientific discoveries of the twentieth century—controlled nuclear fission in 1917, carried out by the New Zealand physicist Ernest Rutherford, and the discovery of the double helix structure of DNA by the American James Watson and the Englishman Francis Crick in 1953.

It is true that Oxford made its own scientific contribution in 1938 with Ernest Chain's creation of synthetic penicillin in a lab on South Parks Road, just down the street from Rhodes House, the headquarters of the Rhodes Scholarships. But the ambience at Cambridge was generally more rationalistic and scientific and with the work of John Maynard Keynes in applied economic theory in the 1930s, Cambridge exerted an enormous influence on social policy in the Anglophone world.

Oxford was the home of classical scholarship, linguistic philosophy, literary studies, and medieval history—and of dreaming in a kind of late Victorian neo-romantic manner. Since the 1880s Oxford had been strongly committed to the British Empire and served as a training ground for its officials. In 1954 it was still doing so.

In 1954 Oxford consisted of some thirty colleges for men and only four for women—coeducation did not come until the 1970s, when Rhodes Scholarships were also opened to women. More than at Cambridge, the strength, power, and wealth of Oxford was concentrated in the autonomous undergraduate colleges rather than in the loosely structured university that existed to sponsor scientific research and give D.Phil.'s, until the 1950s mostly to foreigners.

In the Oxford humanities academic careers were usually based on performance in "the Schools," the formidable undergraduate final exams, rather than on subsequent graduate work, which still had a connotation in 1954 of being for losers in the Schools, foreigners, and Rhodes scholars. To gain tenure as a Fellow or Tutor of Balliol or Magdalen College or one of the other four or five prestigious and wealthy colleges was just as dignified an academic post for most dons as a university chair. Personal qualities of wit, charm, good family, and physical beauty still counted heavily in selection of a new Fellow by the existing community of Fellows.

Once in a while an exotic Jew like Isaiah Berlin was chosen or a brilliant one like the legal theorist H. L. A. Hart, but Jewish representation on the Oxford faculty was tiny. On the other hand, there were only three hundred thousand Jews in the whole country, congregated in the suburbs of Manchester and in North London and engaged mostly in retail trades.

The ambience of Oxford had been damaged after 1910 by the development there of a huge motor car industry in Cowley, a principal suburb. It was as if Princeton were relocated to Detroit. This made the old town noisy, crowded, and expensive. I have never understood why the University did not block this unfortunate intrusion, but possibly the dons were bought off by the automobile magnates. It happens.

On the other hand, the enlarged population allowed Oxford in the late 1950s to be a vibrant center for original and touring theater and to support an excellent art film house where I spent at least two afternoons a week, devouring Cadbury chocolates and watching French films. Thus I avoided engaging like the other Rhodes scholars in what Cecil Rhodes had called "healthy, manly, outdoor sports." I did once turn out for the college rugby team. The burly South Africans beat me up.

All institutions in Britain were painfully harmed by the loss of three-quarters of a million young men lost in the First World War, the greatest disaster in English history after the Black Death of the fourteenth century. Oxford had suffered more than any other community. The beautiful and clever young men of gentry background were the core of its student body and younger faculty and they had all but disappeared into the charnel house of the Allied lines in France.

The Great Depression hit Britain very hard and augmented the pessimistic, almost nihilistic ambience, left over from World War I. While Britain suffered less than half the military casualties in the Second World War than between 1914 and 1918, the second German War had a devastating impact on the civilian population, causing not only destruction from the air but a general malaise from poverty and hunger. The socialists who came to power in 1945 mistakenly extended wartime austerity and overregulation of daily life in order to finance the massive welfare state that they introduced, thereby assuring the long-term decline of the British economy.

British biochemists invented synthetic penicillin but they had to turn to American pharmaceutical companies for the capital investment to bring antibiotics to market. In the 1950s British aeronautical engineers produced the first long distance passenger jet airliner, but it was not commercially feasible. Because of the strength and militancy of labor unions, backed by the socialist government, there was a general incapacity for industrial expansion and technological innovation. The great British ship-manufacturing industry all but disappeared. In 1914 Britain had the largest auto-manufacturing industry in the world next to the United States. By 1980 except for high end luxury cars, the indigenous British auto industry had disappeared and the best-selling car in Britain itself was the Nissan.

British academics, far from lamenting this lugubrious story, contributed to it by their overwhelming loyalty to the political left. When in the late 1980s Prime Minister Margaret Thatcher—who had tried desperately if belatedly to liberate the British market economy from socialism—was nominated for an honorary degree from Oxford, the faculty voted down the proposal.

After 1945 a more intense positivism, empiricism, a sour ungenerous spirit descended on Oxford. Its dreamers did not all disappear—the great medievalist Richard Southern was one—but the faculty as a whole were more heavyset and mean-spirited than before 1914. The head of the History Faculty in the thirties and early forties was Sir Maurice Powicke, a dwarf with a big head who was imported from the grubby dry-as-dust History Department at the University of Manchester, something that would never have happened in the good old Edwardian days.

Alongside Southern the most brilliant historian on the Oxford faculty in the 1950s was A. J. P. Taylor who wrote—for the public at large—on modern diplomacy, politics, and war. A Fellow of Magdalen, he applied again and again for a chair but was turned down by his inferior, jealous colleagues. Finally Taylor left in disgust for London to be the official biographer of the press magnate Lord Beaverbrook and to get rich in journalism. Nobody at Oxford cared. It was a place that had lost its spirit and in my view has never regained it.

Everything went wrong for me in Oxford. The Oxford I imagined no longer existed, if it ever had outside a Max Beerbohm or Dorothy Sayers novel. World War II had not yet ended at Oxford in 1954. It was still a world of gray austerity, as if the German bombs were still dropping on London. The grocery shops were full of good food but the food at Oriel College where I lived was inedible. I survived by buying sandwiches at Marks and Spencer's department store and once a week on Saturday nights eating a splendid but moderately priced meal in the dining room of the Oxford railway hotel. The bathroom facilities at Oriel were abysmal. The nearest toilet to my suite was two flights down;

the nearest shower two blocks away. The Oriel dons struck me as a sodden mass of lazy and pompous alcoholics.

The college operated in a maddeningly inefficient manner. Instead of installing running water on each floor of the student residence, a "scout," an aged manservant, entered each morning and brought a pitcher of hot water and looked around for a used chamber pot to take out. This had been done since the residence was built in the seventeenth century; the routine never changed. Centuries of sanitary technology were ignored. So was the current food market. In my fourteen weeks at Oriel, I was never once served an orange or citrus juice for breakfast. A hundred yards from the college gate cheap Spanish oranges overflowed the grocery stalls. In the whole college of three hundred students there was one phone for student use. I saw that Britain had actually lost the War. The British would easily be overtaken by the Germans whom they had ostensibly defeated.

The decrepitude of the Bodleian Library, with one of the three or four largest collections in the world, was unbelievable. There was no card catalogue, only huge scrapbooks into which slips of bibliographical paper had been pasted in roughly alphabetical order. Many times the slips entered in handwriting before the 1920s had become illegible so it was impossible to order the book by its call number. If one came to Bodleian's main reading room after 11:00 A.M. in term, all the seats were taken.

To relieve oneself in the Bodleian, one had to go down three flights, cross a courtyard, and find a tiny toilet behind a door marked "School of Semitic Languages." All these imbecilities and inconveniences had been cemented into a subculture that identified them with academic culture, making them sacrosanct and inevitable.

From the start I was in the bad graces of Sir Edgar Williams (then, before his knighthood, simply E. T.), the Warden of Rhodes House and administrator of the scholarship program. Williams was a Balliol history don before the War; he published one article, on the British cabinet system, which was all wrong. He had a good war, rising to be General Sir Bernard Montgomery's chief of intelligence after D-day. It was well known that Montgomery's intelligence was bad, resulting in needless mortalities of thousands of soldiers, including my uncle.

The sinecure of the Wardenship of Rhodes House was Sir Edgar's reward after 1945. At my entry interview in September 1954, conducted while he was decanting port, Williams told me that he did not approve of my selection to Cecil Rhodes' exalted company of young men (no women until 1972). I was no athlete; I came from an obscure family; I had no interest in politics. What kind of leader, what kind of a superman that Rhodes had envisaged, was I? Medieval history, what had that to do with the purposes of the Rhodes Trust, designed to foster men of power and wealth like old Cecil himself?

Sir Edgar did not specifically mention something that I felt deeply and thought he was implying. I was only the third Jewish Rhodes scholar to be chosen from the Province of Manitoba in the half-century existence of the Rhodes program. The first had been David Golden, a war hero, and later a distinguished and much revered judge. The second was Alan Gotlieb, the son of the second richest Jew in Winnipeg. Alan was a man of fastidious taste and elegant dress. He was already in 1954 an Oxford law don and was later to be an important and long-running Canadian ambassador to Washington.

Compared to these giants I was an obscure silly nerd, a man without parts. I had been selected only because the chairman of the Manitoba

Rhodes selection committee, the historian William L. Morton, had worn down his colleagues on the committee on my behalf because he thought from Strayer's and Mommsen's letters of reference I might be a genius.

I deeply disappointed Bill Morton because I was gone from Oxford by March 1955, a record failure and a crashing embarrassment back home. Warden Williams' initial negative assessment of me turned out, in his eyes, to be thoroughly prescient. I played on no athletic team; I turned down the Queen's invitation to her garden party at Buckingham Palace, unprecedented bad behavior for a Rhodes scholar. I turned down several invitations arranged by Rhodes House to spend weekends at gentry country houses. At Christmas, Williams caught me sneaking out of the Bodleian Library after a day of research whereas I should have been touring France and Italy.

Above all I created a row by quarreling with my supervisor, R. W. Southern (later Sir Richard, Chichele Professor of Medieval History, President of St. John's College, Oxford). This incompatibility with my romantic hero Southern was a shock to me and made my continuance at Oxford unbearable.

Like not a few Oxbridge dons of his wartime generation, Dick Southern was a split person. He was a radical as a writer (although no other book of his approached the academically subversive humanist tone of *The Making of the Middle Ages*), but a social conformist in everyday life. He was content with the dry positivism, the extreme empiricism, the anti-intellectuality, the tedious cultural conservatism of the Oxford history faculty as long as he could play house romantic with impunity. He was a tall, handsome man with a melodious voice who resembled Laurence Olivier. He was not interested in, indeed shrank from, producing radical romantic copies of himself among his graduate students.

He had announced an intellectual revolution coming down the tracks in medieval studies, but when the train arrived at the station, he got into the dons' club car and exchanged pleasantries with them over sherry. Misguided, naïve young people like myself who took his published ideas seriously and wanted to turn them into a revolutionary academic program he turned away from with a shudder to resume his joshing with the dons. After three or four interviews with him I felt what Robert Browning said of William Wordsworth: "For only a hand-ful of silver he left us. / For only a ribbon to stick in his coat."

At the time I blamed Southern's split behavior mostly on his wife, the widow of an R. A. F. war hero. She was the head of the upscale Oxford Bach Society, an ambitious woman set on becoming Lady as Dick became Sir. But this was a narrow and misogynist view of Southern's temperament on my part. He was a book man, a teacher, and a writer, but he sensed mortal danger to himself if he became any sort of activist trying to lift the Oxford history faculty out of its postwar dust, timidity, and torpor. Of course he was right to sense this danger. If he did not prevail in a revolution, he would be destroyed by the dons.

The Regius Professor and therefore nominal head of the history faculty was Vivian H. Galbraith, who had the mind of the second-rate archivist he had been for twenty years. He admitted to me that he could not read a word of German. He was completely out of touch with the vast German literature on the medieval church. Galbraith was not without a certain vulgar charm. He was a strong socialist, which is why Labor Party Prime Minister Clement Attlee had made him Regius Professor, a chair that was a gift of the Crown. Galbraith looked like a

Lancashire farmer dressed up for Sunday church. He swore like a longshoreman. For me to have an interview with him, I had to enter his "rooms" (office) at Oriel a half an hour before my appointment and light the coal fire. He regarded Southern as an exotic flower in the rocky pedestrian soil of Oxford postwar historiography, to be protected but not to be taken seriously.

Galbraith and Southern insisted I attend the two courses specially designed for entering graduate students in medieval history: Paleography (medieval handwriting) and Diplomatic (document expertise, from the Latin *diploma*, a document).

Paleography was taught to a class of about thirty by Neil Ker, the University Archivist. He was a thin, nervous man who avoided all eye contact with the students. At the first class meeting he went to the blackboard in the shabby, dimly-lit lecture hall, and put an "A" on the board and said "this is how they made an 'A' in the Carolingian era." And so through the alphabet. Rather crude, I thought, but he doesn't want to overwhelm us. Came the second lecture, Ker went to the board, wrote a slightly different "A" and said: "This is how they made an 'A' in the Ottonian era." I got up and left, not to return.

Diplomatic was taught in a seminar room to five students, including me, by Dr. Kathleen Major, Fellow and later Principal of St. Hilda's College, the bourgeois women's college. She was a well put together woman of about fifty. She lectured in a squeaky, high-pitched voice at great speed. The content seemed pretty good, although very elementary and somewhat familiar. She assumed from the start that I was a hick. "This course," she said at the first class, looking straight at me, "is not about international relations."

"I know that, Dr. Major. I am here to learn about medieval documents," I said.

She was a stickler for university rules. We were supposed to wear short black gowns to class—as well as dinner. Frequently I turned up at her class without my silly gown, which distressed her as a sign presumably that I did not respect her exalted academic status of Reader (associate professor) in Diplomatic.

After several warnings that I ignored she exploded, "If you come to class again without your gown, Mr. Cantor, I will call the University Proctors and have you arrested" (under a fourteenth-century statute). I took this as a declaration of war. I went to the Bodleian and got out the two-volume German textbook on the subject of "document-learning" by Harry Bresslau. I had read them for Mommsen's seminar my first semester at Princeton. Sure enough, Major's lectures were lifted right out of Bresslau. She had only changed the examples from Bresslau's German and Italian documents to English ones. Now I went to class with my gown but took no notes. She fell into the trap. "Why are you not taking notes, Mr. Cantor?"

"Because, Dr. Major, I like my Bresslau pure." She flushed deeply; the other students who, of course, could not read German were mystified by this exchange.

As I was recovering later that day from another sodden Oriel lunch of "toad in the hole" (sausage in dough), I was handed a personal message from Dr. Major. "Come to tea today 4:00 P.M." I went to St. Hilda's College and found her suite of rooms. To my surprise the walls were painted white, the floor was covered with good beige carpeting, and the furniture was Danish Modern, still rare and upscale in postwar England. Dr. Major was freshly dressed in a good gray suit and there was a trace of lipstick around her mouth. She was chain-smoking cigarettes. I stuck with my pipe but I accepted tea and cucumber sandwiches. After a few pleasantries ("How different Oxford must be from Princeton!" she expostulated. "A bit," I replied.) she suddenly said with fierce determination: "For twenty years I was a schoolteacher and an archivist. This is the best job I could get at Oxford. I don't know much about the subject, but I am learning. Don't ruin it for me, Mr. Cantor." I promised I would not, but I never went back to her class.

A month later, feasting in the Oxford railway hotel on a lonely Saturday night, I noticed Dr. Major dining in another corner of the underpopulated dining room. I waited for her to invite me to join her. She did not. We both ate alone and in silence, a scene from a Terence Rattigan play. At least Kathleen Major respected—indeed plagiarized—German medieval scholarship.

Southern constantly railed against Ernst Kantorowicz as a decadent German phony. Dick was proud that he helped drive EKA from Oxford in 1938. I told Southern that his approach and attitude toward the Middle Ages were closer to Kantorowicz than he was willing to recognize. The difference between EKA and Sir Richard was, after all, the difference between heavy-handed German romanticism and the more light-fingered English variety. It was the difference between Heine and Byron, between Richard Wagner and Sir Edward Elgar.

This was a message that Dick did not want to hear. Like so many history dons of his wartime generation, he was a cultural nationalist. England was somehow special, intellectually better than Germany or the United States. When I met Dick in 1954 one of the first things he said to me was that he had never been in the United States and would never go there. Later in 1963 he changed his mind and I helped arrange a lecture tour for him. My wife and I took him to the Metropolitan Opera and he stayed overnight in our humble basement apartment on the northern extremity of Manhattan.

His attitude to the Germans and their historiography never changed, however. *The Making of the Middle Ages*, that wonderful book of 1953, is all the more remarkable for having been written by someone who ignored—or possibly could not read—the vast German literature on medieval ecclesiastical culture. Dick did not have a high opinion of David Knowles, the contemporary monastic historian at Cambridge because Knowles was fluent in German and drew heavily on German scholarship.

After five months of tense discussions, Sir Richard and I could not even agree on a topic for my doctoral dissertation, which meant I could not be approved by the history faculty as a research (doctoral) student. From my quandary Strayer's cable in mid-March rescued me with an offer to come back to Princeton and teach. I went to see Southern and asked him what I should do. "By all means accept the Princeton offer. You have no future here. I doubt whether you can ever get an Oxford D.Phil. There is certainly little hope of your getting a teaching job in Britain." He was very glad to be rid of me, before this gauche Canadian cowboy got into a public fight with the history dons and embarrassed Dick.

I immediately went to see Sir Edgar Williams, still busily decanting port in his office. A larger than life-size portrait of Cecil Rhodes in riding costume, in this picture remarkably resembling Hitler, hung behind him. I told E. T. that I was resigning my scholarship as of the coming August 1955 and returning to Princeton to teach. I told him that I wanted to "go down" immediately from Oxford, but also to keep my Rhodes money for the year (paid in four installments). I intended, I said, to live in London and finish the research for my Princeton Ph.D. before I returned to America. "Unprecedented," Sir Edgar said, "but I will take this matter up with the Rhodes Trustees at our meeting next week." A week later he sent me a letter telling me that not only could I do what I wanted now but that the one year's unspent balance of my scholarship money would be reserved for me to come back to England sometime to do research (I did in the summer of 1959, coming with my wife and ten-month-old son, who vomited on Southern when Dick picked him up). The Rhodes Trustees were willing to make a generous concession in order to be rid of me.

In London I lived in a seedy, dirt-cheap residential hotel in the unfashionable Earl's Court section (where Albert Einstein had lived in 1933), ate splendid meals in Pakistani restaurants, worked six days a week in the British Museum Library and its grand Victorian circular reading room (recently abandoned by the Library) and toured every important museum and art gallery in the city. I was happy as a bird.

I should have taken pains and time after defending my Princeton dissertation and getting my Ph.D. to revise and polish it. Instead the book that was published was exactly as it had been as my doctoral dissertation, a very rare occurrence in the humanities.

This was because the main reader of the manuscript for the Princeton University Press was David Knowles, the senior professor of medieval history at Cambridge and as holder of the Regius (royal) chair nominally the head of the whole history faculty. Knowles praised the manuscript to the skies and urged that it be published immediately and without any needed revision. It was like a young physicist being touted by Einstein.

David Knowles was as tempestuous and aggressive a personality as he was an immensely learned scholar and beautiful writer. His first book, on English monasticism from about 900 to the early 13th century, had shaken up the medievalist establishment when it was published by Cambridge University Press in 1940. At that time Knowles was a renegade Benedictine monk living in London with a female Swedish psychiatrist who had helped him while he was seeking psychotherapy at Tavistock Clinic, later to be made famous by R. D. Laing.

Knowles' battle with his abbot, which had led to his running away, was covered up by the papacy because his book on monasticism made him overnight the leading Roman Catholic medievalist. He was allowed to return to the priesthood and was given permanent leave from his abbey. During the War he was invited to join the Cambridge faculty. From the time of publication of my dissertation in 1958 until Knowles' death in 1963, he was my principal academic mentor. One thing that brought us together was joint deep knowledge of German scholarship on the medieval church. A second was a love of biography.

In the summer of 1959, I spoke at an international conference of historians in London at Knowles' invitation and with the pugnacious little monk chairing the session in front of two hundred medievalists. When a woman don from Cambridge asked me tough questions in the public discussion after my paper, Knowles rose to my defense. This scene is remarkably anticipated in the only good novel ever written about a medieval historian, Angus Wilson's *Anglo-Saxon Attitudes*. At the time in 1959 Wilson worked in the British Museum Library (back in 1955 he had let me sneak into the Reading Room of the Library thirty minutes before its daily official opening). He was possibly present that July day when Nora Chadwick rose and shrieked at me, "What about the

Welsh Church?" and I stood struck dumb at the podium until the undaunted Knowles rescued me.

Southern had a low opinion of Knowles' work, which he considered too Germanic. Knowles thought that Southern was at best a middle-weight and too caught up in the Oxford donnish lifestyle.

Southern was certainly not present to hear my paper on that day in July 1959. After my presentation Knowles took my wife and me on a walking tour through the Chelsea part of London. We lunched together and then, and in subsequent letters, he tried to guide me in my scholarly career. But I only heard his praise of me, not his advice which would have sentenced me to a lifetime of breathing archival dust.

I was also very happy professionally during the first three of my six years at Columbia (1960–66). I was immensely popular with the students, women as well as men. I completed and published the first version of what was to become in 1994 *The Civilization of the Middle Ages*. In all it has gone through forty printings and has become the all-time best-selling survey of medieval history published in the United States. This widely read book is a memorial of my good times at Columbia.

When old King's College of the eighteenth century moved from what is now the site of Rockefeller Center in the early years of the twentieth century, following the new IRT subway line to Morningside Heights, Columbia was refounded as primarily a graduate school, imitating Johns Hopkins. When I came there in the fall of 1960 it was still a place of great intellectual seriousness and open to new ideas, although in retrospect many people think Columbia had peaked around 1950.

On my first day on the campus I sat down for lunch in the Faculty Club with the sociologists Robert Merton and Paul Lazarsfeld and the next week with the anthropologists Marvin Harris and Margaret Mead. I sat in on lectures by Meyer Schapiro on art history, Lionel Trilling on literature, and Jacques Barzun on intellectual history that were breathtaking in their sweep and originality. I sat for weeks on end in the wonderful Burgess-Carpenter Library where multiple copies of the important recent books in every field and discipline—including my Princeton doctoral dissertation—were available on the open shelves. Thus I gained deep immersion in the beginning of the new academic culture.

In my first three years at Columbia I read my way through much of Freud's corpus in the Strachey translation and three volumes of Jung in the Bollingen edition. I mastered the work of Max Weber, most of it still in difficult German. I became interested in anthropology of which until that time I had read scarcely a line (Princeton, in fact, then had no separate Anthropology Department). I had a very good tutor, the brilliant Marxist Marvin Harris who later became Chairman of the Columbia Anthropology Department, the first one in that discipline to be founded in the United States.

I also learned a lot of anthropology simply by being the external examiner on oral comprehensive exams and dissertation defenses of doctoral candidates. Columbia had an unusual system of the Dean of the Graduate School selecting a professor from another department to add to the four examiners from within the doctoral candidate's department. What to do with a superfluous medievalist like me? I was occasionally privileged to sit in on exams and dissertation defenses of the English Department's medieval students. That is how I discovered the marvelous historian and critic of medieval literature, Robert Hanning—I was his external examiner. I got appointed to an examining committee in the Department of Statistics—I who had trouble adding up four figures. I thought the student was a genius. It turned out he was very marginal and the departmental examiners split two to two. I had to cast the deciding vote and I naturally voted to pass the student. The department chairman cussed me out and wrote an indignant letter to the dean.

So I was tried out in anthropology exams and that went well for both sides. That is where I saw Margaret Mead in action. She held an appointment at the Museum of Natural History and was an adjunct professor at Columbia. She was a portly, formidable woman who would come in hobbling on her cane. She always seemed to be in an angry mood. Her questions to the student revealed an extraordinarily subtle mind at work. Mead was especially hard on woman candidates. I remember her saying at one dissertation defense by a woman candidate after the student had withdrawn to let the examiners confer: "This woman has been in the field too long. She has lost touch with civilization."

I heard Claude Lévi-Strauss's name mentioned for the first time in anthropology exams—by no means always favorably—and I read the French edition of *Tristes Tropiques* (1955). I realized immediately that here was the greatest behavioral scientist of this century after Freud. I discovered that during the War Lévi-Strauss was a refugee professor in New York City. In the summer of 1945 he taught an introductory course to Barnard women. I have always thought that would make a good drama.

One of the consequences of my learning anthropology at Columbia was that when it became fashionable for historians—especially feminist historians—to claim in the 1970s and 1980s that they were joining history and anthropology, I knew enough to perceive if they were well informed or just spouting fashionable nonsense. About fifty-fifty.

In my first three years, by Dick Morris's arrangement, I taught a two-semester course on medieval culture at Barnard College to a class of forty women and ten men (who crossed Broadway from Columbia College). It was the best teaching experience of my life. The Barnard students—half of them upper middle-class New York metropolitan Jewish women—were marvelous. Like many college teachers, the better the students, the better my performance.

Each Monday, Wednesday, and Friday I had a ritual: at 6:00 A.M. leaving my drab apartment in the northern extremity of Manhattan or the west Bronx, emerging from the IRT subway at 116th and Broadway to pick up three sugar donuts and a small black coffee at Chock Full of Nuts on that corner, then an hour in my office in Fayerweather Hall, one of Stanford White's monumental Italian Romanesque, but now decaying buildings. Then across Broadway again to my classroom at Barnard to put a detailed outline of the lecture on the board, then fifty minutes of lecturing, often coming up with ideas in the heat of discourse that had lain somewhere below my consciousness.

Among the many remarkable Barnard students were Elaine Robison, a phenomenal Latinist from the Upper West Side, and the first woman to get a Ph.D. in medieval history—with Strayer—at Princeton; Carol Berkin, a Jewish woman from the deep South who got a Ph.D. in American colonial history with Richard B. Morris, wrote prolifically in that field and also became a pioneering psychohistorian, undergoing professional training as a lay analyst; and Zane Berzins, perhaps the most brilliant of all, who now heads the public relations department at one of the CUNY colleges. Among the unforgettable students at

Columbia College in my legal history course were Sanford Greenberg, a legally blind student from Buffalo who got a Ph.D. in politics from Harvard and became a highly successful venture capitalist in Washington D.C. and Kenneth Lipper, lawyer, deputy mayor of New York, and multimillionaire investment broker and philanthropist.

I gained deep immersion in the social and behavioral sciences and enormously expanded my intellectual horizons. It was my time of academic epiphany. One day Lionel Trilling stopped me as I walked across the campus. He had read my history of medieval civilization and he thought it a good book, he said. I was on Cloud Nine.

Another day there was a knock at my office door and a handsome, slim young man came in and introduced himself as Terence Hopkins, one of the Sociology Department's two rising stars in Robert Merton's wide ranging kind of historical sociology (the other stellar figure was Immanuel Wallerstein). The sociologists had been watching me, Hopkins told me. Wouldn't I like to apply for a research grant controlled by a committee that Hopkins chaired? Of course I would. I got the grant.

I seemed to be on my way to academic stardom at Columbia, in a place that I respected and loved. Then things started to go wrong. I became subject to fiscal constraints and to collegial backbiting, two chronic Columbia adverse conditions.

I simply could not raise a family in expensive New York on what Columbia was paying me. Dick Morris told me that since the Columbia History Department was founded around 1905, a full professor's salary had risen from $7,000 to only $11,000 which meant in real terms, salaries in 1963 were less than half of what they had been when Columbia opened its magnificent Stanford White doors on Morningside Heights.

Many of the history faculty had deals going to raise income: textbooks, journalism (Dick Morris himself supervised the production of a recording of American Revolution songs), and for bottom feeders like myself moonlighting on other campuses. Twice I taught at the uptown or downtown branches of Yeshiva University. The subway rides alone exhausted me. My constant worrying about and grubbing for money was demoralizing and further damaged my fragile marriage.

Under Nicholas Murray Butler as president for four decades earlier in the century, Columbia had been different, because Butler got rich people from old New York families, like the sugar monopolists the Havemeyers, to sit on the Board of Trustees and lavish their well-matured money on the university. The Columbia presidents who came after Butler, including Dwight Eisenhower, were lax about fund-raising, the most important responsibility of the president of a private university, especially from the new Jewish postwar billionaire families. Only in the 1960s was a Jewish plutocrat finally appointed to the Columbia Board of Trustees; he promptly endowed a new engineering building.

But in the 1960s it was still a matter of too little and too late. A lot of New York Jewish money that could have easily been solicited for Columbia went instead to the new Jewish-sponsored Brandeis University in a Boston suburb. Columbia's endowment stagnated while its operating costs skyrocketed.

By 1961 money was so scarce on Morningside Heights that Provost Jacques Barzun tried to save a little by cutting off off-campus telephone service from professors' offices. For a few embarrassing months Nobel and Pulitzer Prize winning faculty lined up with others, clutching their dimes, to use in pay phones on the ground floor of Stanford White's palatial faculty office buildings. When I taught in the summer session in 1962, offices and lecture rooms were still not air-conditioned.

The second problem endemic to the Columbia History Department was clique and cabal formation, partisan and personal departmental politics—especially after strongman Richard Morris ceased being chairman in 1963—and backbiting, going as far as taking vengeance on graduate students because their mentors were the powerless ones. Among the faculty I found myself increasingly isolated.

John Mundy, the other medievalist, launched a campaign against me: I was not a scholar, he claimed. I should not be teaching in the graduate school and supervising dissertations. I developed a swelled head as a result of my great success as a teacher of undergraduates at Columbia. I did not accord John Mundy sufficient respect. He was a fine scholar and a good trainer of graduate students. He found my arrogance insufferable. Mundy was joined in assaulting me by Peter Gay, who was angry at me for my upfront role in blocking the appointment of a friend of his (who would, if appointed, have taken my precious legal history course away from me). Gay was close to the most influential departmental faculty (after Morris withdrew his presence to stay home in Westchester County and make money on publishing deals)—Jacques Barzun and Richard Hofstadter.

I found myself increasingly marginalized and demoted to the scrub team. I was assigned now to the hellhole of the evening adult education program.

I explored offers from elsewhere—first from the new campus of the University of California at Santa Cruz, and then from Brandeis University in Waltham, Massachusetts, a Boston suburb. I foolishly turned down the Santa Cruz offer after spending five weeks out there in the summer of 1964 overscrupulously trying to estimate the future of that emerging campus. I decided finally that California was another country in which I would not get my bearings.

I accepted the Brandeis job and left in the summer of 1966 to live in Lexington, Massachusetts. John Mundy celebrated. "We'll never invite him back," he cackled in the Faculty Club. He was right. Mundy had an exceptional student and pioneering feminist medievalist, the Hungarian countess Suzanne Wemple, whom he wanted to place in the Barnard job, and succeeded in doing so, with me out of the way.

In 1997 my editor at HarperCollins told me he was also editing a book by the now venerable, long retired, but still productive Jacques Barzun, who had requested that I read and comment on a chapter dealing with the Middle Ages in a book he was writing. I did so. The chapter was out-of-date and I told Barzun that in my written comments. The chapter, not surprisingly, was redolent of the world of Shepherd Clough and Garret Mattingly, good in its day but long superseded. In thanking me for my critique, Barzun's letter expressed regret that I had been underappreciated at Columbia in the old days. He was right.

The slovenly disorder of Columbia in 1966 is demonstrated by a peculiar incident that occurred in May, when I had already packed up the books in my office, bought a house in Lexington, and was preparing to leave for Massachusetts three weeks later. The dean of Columbia College, the brilliant political scientist David Truman, suddenly summoned me to his office. He had just learned that I was leaving and greatly regretted it because he knew how successful my legal history course was (they never found a successful replacement for me). If I would rescind my resignation and kiss off Brandeis, Truman said he would raise a million dollars from a private benefactor and set me up in my own institute.

I sat in silence and looked at him. Where was he when I needed him? Finally I said it was too late; I was going to Brandeis. Of course I was a fool.

I went to Brandeis so that my family could live a comfortable suburban middle-class life; because Brandeis promised me *carte blanche* in the way of resources to create a new graduate program in comparative history along the lines of the emerging new culture; and because I gave up all hope of getting another job in the Ivy League.

In 1963 before leaving office as chair of the department, Dick Morris suddenly started talking to me in an unusually benign manner. One morning I was startled to find Shepherd Clough entering my office to exchange pleasantries about nothing. Something was afoot and Morris finally confessed to me that the Columbia professor emeritus of medieval science, Lynn Thorndike, had chaired the Harvard ad hoc external committee on appointing to tenure Giles Constable, a Harvard Ph.D. then teaching in Iowa.

The external committee, as Thorndike told Morris, had turned down Constable and recommended me to the Harvard prexy for the medievalist position. But Constable was the son of the head of the Boston art museum; his wife owned a big share of General Electric; and the senior medievalist at Harvard, Charles H. Taylor (he of the famous two articles in his lifetime portfolio, one wrong and the other un-readable) had whipped up anti-Semitic Brahmin frenzy to bring in Constable and keep me out. The Harvard president gave in.

But for a wonderful week or so Thorndike was telling his friends in the Columbia History Department to make nice to me as I was about to get a tenured full professor offer from Harvard. When Constable's appointment was confirmed, the grand patrons at Columbia withdrew their protection of me and allowed Mundy and Gay to return to their favorite game of disparaging me and flunking my graduate students.

I was deeply hurt that the medievalist Jewish historian in the department, Gerson Cohen, whom I thought was a friend of mine, joined Mundy and Gay in turning against me. Cohen, later Chancellor of the Jewish Theological Seminary, stopped talking to me. I thought that Brandeis would be a salubrious environment after these bad days on Morningside Heights when I went home at 10:00 P.M. from my scurvy adult education class weeping on the subway to the abominable Bronx.

The denouement of my Columbia years was all the more bitter because I sensed that in spite of Columbia's fiscal problems and its inert presidents, it was the site where—along with perhaps Berkeley, Yale, and Chicago—a new academic culture was starting to take shape that was going to leave behind Princeton's post-Edwardian, Oxford-imitating humanism. Something more deeply intellectual and complex and in tune with vanguard behavioral theory was emerging at Columbia, led by Meyer Schapiro in art history, Lionel Trilling and the young medievalist Robert Hanning in the English Department, Barzun and Richard Hofstadter in history, and Robert Merton the historical sociologist and his acolytes Terence Hopkins and Immanuel Wallerstein.

It did not take the dean at Brandeis, Leonard Levy, and the chair of the History Department, Morton Keller, both first class American legal and political historians, long to realize my situation when we sat down to talk after they invited me to their modest campus in Waltham, Massachusetts, in 1965. They realized that I definitely wanted out from

Morningside Heights even though I drank deeply from—and contributed to—its innovative academic culture.

Levy and Keller painted an ideal picture for me—I could leave Columbia and at Brandeis create a graduate program in my own image to be called "Comparative History" and it would have all the resources I needed; just write my own ticket. I was getting due recognition at last!

Thus Brandeis offered me the moon. When I got to Brandeis in the summer of 1966 and had moved into our comfortable new house in Lexington, ten miles from the campus, I discovered that the moon was made of green cheese. Except for a couple of graduate assistantships there were no resources for my Comparative History Program: no library, no office space, no secretary, no research, travel, and publication fund.

I knew I was doomed the last week of August 1966 when I went to the director of the Brandeis University Library to complain that a dozen books on medieval history that I told the library several months earlier to buy for my upcoming fall graduate course were still not listed in the card catalogue. The librarian smiled and took me down into the basement of the library building. There he showed me some twenty thousand book order cards from faculty in the past three years, my order slips among them, that he had backfiled simply because he had no money to order the books. "But didn't Dean Levy tell you that mine was a special case?"

"I never heard about you from Dean Levy." My optimistic little balloon deflated instantly.

Leonard Levy as dean had made glowing promises to me; Mickey Keller, smiling as always, had backed him up. They admired me; they were well intentioned. They did what was always done at Brandeis— make commitments and then go to the Big Daddy of the campus,

Abraham Sachar, founding president of the university since 1948, with two more years to run until his retirement, and ask the old magician to manufacture the program funding. Somehow Sachar always came through and that is why Brandeis had a remarkably good faculty for such a new and small and physically humble place. It deserved at best to be slotted with Wesleyan or Amherst but was aiming to be Yale or Princeton.

Somehow Abe Sachar with the ethics of a used car dealer and the skills of a Middle Eastern rug salesman found the resources to recruit and keep more or less happy a crew of stellar academics. He would put the touch on some Manhattan Jewish millionaire with fresh money, whom Columbia ignored as too uncouth, if necessary telling the donor that the gift was slotted for X when it was really used for Y in a perpetual shell game. He would rename an existing building for the donor's family covering up the name of a previous donor long tapped out. He would modify the menu in the Faculty Dining Club, reducing the quality of the corned beef—he would come up with something. This time, for Cantor's Comparative History Program he just sighed and held out his open palms. He was exhausted, worn out from twenty years of playing tricks and fictionalizing budgets to fool the University Trustees, of spending the same dollar twice or thrice, of secretly going to banks and running up huge debts on unpaid loans to the University.

He was also prescient. Like a Las Vegas gambler with bad cards at 4:00 A.M., Sachar sensed the game was over.

A year after I got to Brandeis, while Leonard Levy now back in the history department as chair, and a new dean, the philosopher Peter Diamandopoulos, a wily aristocratic Cretan Gentile, were still pressing Abe Sachar to fulfill the rash promises that Levy and Keller had made to me, the Six Day War broke out in the Middle East. The president's telephone line burned up with calls from donors who had already pledged big gifts or paid the first installments on them, saying sorry, Abe, but Israel, poor little embattled Israel, comes first. We are wiring the millions destined for Brandeis to Tel Aviv instead. In one week Abe Sachar reportedly lost fifty million dollars in pledges and gifts. Brandeis was a dead duck financially and my carefully structured graduate program that was going to revolutionize training in the discipline was now a useless piece of paper.

Abe Sachar withdrew from his customary very public view on the campus and told the Trustees to find a new president. They did forthwith. Morris B. Abrams, a courtly New York lawyer, a Rhodes scholar, a former southerner who had played a historic role in the civil rights movement, a man of wit, courage, and learning, became president. His first day on the campus he was allowed to discover that technically Brandeis was bankrupt; its debts far exceeded its assets. Within two years, after painful exchanges with the Trustees who had deceived him, Abrams was back practicing corporate law at Paul, Weiss, and Rifkind in Manhattan. The strains of his disastrous Brandeis presidency ruined his marriage.

By 1970 Leonard Levy also departed to become chairman of the History Department and to fill a distinguished chair in history at Claremont in California. He merited such recognition after winning the Pulitzer Prize in history with my scholarly help. He gave as his lame excuse for hastily departing Brandeis after two decades that his chronically ill wife needed daily outdoor swimming facilities as part of her therapy.

In the summer of 1970, I departed too, my wife and children unhappily accompanying me to the small city of Binghamton on the Susquehanna River in the southern tier of upstate New York, where the northern tip of the Catskills meets the Appalachians. There was being rapidly developed a University Center (doctoral-level school) of the new megalopolis in higher education, Governor Nelson Rockefeller's State University of New York, with thirty-two campuses, four of them University Centers. Here in Binghamton was slated to arise if not a new Berkeley, at least a new San Diego or Santa Barbara campus. I was to be Distinguished Professor of Medieval Studies, a superstar academic level, and chairman of the feverishly expanding History Department.

Binghamton had been the original home of IBM until around 1965, when most of IBM's executive and research personnel were switched overnight to Westchester County, leaving a glutted real estate market in the now chronically depressed city of one hundred thousand people. I bought dirt-cheap a magnificent ten-room house, which somewhat pacified my family's distress at being uprooted from Lexington, Massachusetts. Summers we rented a lakefront cottage fifty miles away in the most beautiful of the Finger Lakes, Skaneatles. I even bought a boat, which I never learned how to operate, but my son did. In Binghamton my daughter and son learned to ski and also to ride horseback with a proficiency I never knew back in Canada. My wife began her professional studies in art history, which led to a graduate degree in that arcane subject from the University of Chicago in 1978 and then to a career in publishing. My son became the best ice hockey player in the county. The personal rewards of Binghamton were great; basement apartments in the Bronx were long forgotten.

I was personally delighted by my appointment as SUNY Distinguished Professor, which required approval by a secret committee selected by the American Historical Association. Some years later I discovered that the luminary on the assenting committee was Robert R. Palmer, the French Revolution scholar and Director of Graduate

Studies in History at Princeton who used to growl at me to work harder (no student ever worked hard enough to satisfy Robespierre, as the graduate students called Palmer— he was famous for throwing graduate students out of the school in the middle of the semester). He had sat on my doctoral orals in 1953, puffing the abominable cheap pipe tobacco that he favored and saying nothing.

The Six Day War ravished Brandeis and the slaughter was finessed by the Columbia Trustees suddenly realizing around 1970 that the solution to Columbia's fiscal woes was to solicit fresh Jewish money. The chairman of Brandeis's Board of Trustees, Leonard Wein, a real estate plutocrat and a graduate of Columbia College, resigned as soon as the Columbia Trustees offered him a slot on their hitherto WASPish Board. He made a huge donation to build a new football stadium for the Columbia Lions, money that could have floated my ambitious graduate program, plus a couple dozen others. Every time I read about the Columbia Lions losing another game at Wein Stadium, I painfully remember my useless years at Brandeis.

Looking back at the Brandeis phenomenon three decades later, after the wounds have turned to scars, I can see that there are two lessons to be learned from the Abe Sachar saga. One is well known —that Jews have a lot of *chutzpah* and have been conditioned by their hazardous history to undertake well-nigh-impossible projects against the severest odds. In the case of Brandeis, they failed; in the case of Israel, a similar harebrained scheme, they seemed to have succeeded although the story continues.

Secondly, and not so obvious, the Brandeis story teaches that very good new universities *could* be created in a couple of decades in the second half of the twentieth century. There are always very good academics or public intellectuals around looking for an academic roost (such as in Brandeis's case Herbert Marcuse and Max Lerner, persons of great intellectual stature in philosophy and political sociology, respectively) who can be recruited to undertake bold things that are better, in a creative way, than was found in the traditionally elite institutions.

The problem is that after a couple of decades, bold and imaginative ventures have to be solidified with deep resources or things will fall apart. There is an old Yiddish expression for over-commitment, *"Er vill tanzen aff alle chasenes,"* he wants to dance at all weddings. That is the Sachar and Brandeis story.

To some extent it is also the Binghamton story. A relatively new campus that in 1970 had apparently unlimited state-provided resources found its income starting to retrench by 1975. Ten years later the campus budget had shrunk by 20 percent and the once promising campus had become—as a graduate school and research center—a thing of shreds and patches. It remained in effect a good and wonderfully cheap undergraduate college in the Catskills, an academic version of Grossingers or the Concord resort hotels thirty-five miles south of Binghamton.

Rockefeller finally departed after the most gigantic state-funded building program since the pyramids. In 1975 after Rockefeller's departure from Albany came three governors in a row, Hugh Carey, Mario Cuomo, and George Pataki who were no friends of the State University of New York. They regarded its value and its priority for state funding to be well below that of the state's prison system.

Rockefeller had in a way contributed to bringing on this evaluation. His Draconian drug laws so exploded the state's prison population that the succeeding governors had to undertake a massive program of prison building to accommodate the victims of them. The three governors found the billions of dollars for prison expansion in the SUNY budget.

Furthermore, beginning with the Irish Catholic Hugh Carey, who was married to a brazen Greek Orthodox real estate queen from Chicago, the governors gave heed to the long-standing complaints of the state's private colleges, especially the many Catholic schools, that taxpayer-funded SUNY was unfair competition in the state's student recruitment pool.

In the 1970s strenuous efforts were also made to reduce the number of doctoral programs in the SUNY system by using unfriendly academic evaluation teams from other states. A Harvard professor, Ernest May, headed the history doctoral program evaluations on the SUNY University Center campuses. He was well paid to do a hatchet job on the SUNY history programs. The Harvard professor and his committee put the Binghamton history doctoral program on a deadly three-year probation by claiming the Binghamton library's history collection was inadequate. Then it was brought to his attention by me that the Cornell University library, forty minutes on the highway from Binghamton, was a state facility to which Binghamton students were supposed to have full access. The Harvard professor didn't earn the fee he was paid— embarrassingly he had to retract his hatchet job on Binghamton.

Whether the SUNY system could ever have reached the level of Berkeley, UCLA, and the California system that Rockefeller intended cannot be known. It would have taken another fifteen years of priority funding and good administrative leadership to find this out. But the liberal Democrat governors Carey and Cuomo and the conservative Republican Pataki made sure it didn't happen.

Because the fiscal assault on the SUNY system was a bipartisan gubernatorial venture, the decline of the SUNY doctoral campuses received very little media attention. The long-suffering taxpayers of New York were never given the option of choosing between more prisons and high quality research universities. Carey, Cuomo, and Pataki thereby expressed their contempt for the voters of New York.

A big problem with the SUNY system as a whole was the University Center at Stony Brook in Suffolk County, Long Island. It was a brand new campus built from the ground up in the 1970s at enormous expense in the genteel village of Stony Brook (whose citizens did not want their gentry environment changed by a state campus) ten miles from the federal nuclear laboratory at Brookhaven. The founding and long-serving president of Stony Brook was a reputable physicist, as was his vice president. They envisaged Stony Brook as a science- and medicine-focused campus, a sort of New York version of MIT, only better. The undergraduate liberal arts college at Stony Brook was pitifully neglected in the interests of building up a stellar scientific research campus that would coordinate with Brookhaven. No one ever gave Stony Brook this ambitious mandate; it was the province of its own executives.

In the SUNY system the Central Administration in Albany was weak and passive. It tended to let each campus do what it wanted; there was nothing of what might be called central planning, which marked the growth of the California University system. Stony Brook, in spite of its lavish funding, consistently overspent its budget. It was quietly bailed out year after year by the Central Administration in Albany, at the cost of unbalancing the whole SUNY budget, even before Carey and his successors retrenched it.

The Stony Brook fiscal mess fell hardest on the Binghamton campus, which had no science or medical programs to speak of and was trying to focus on excellence in the humanities and behavioral sciences. But this development in turn required enormous library resources, which were held back in the interests of Stony Brook's bloated budget and cost overruns.

Until 1976 Binghamton even lacked a library building. When one was finally opened, it was inadequate and its book collection budget was about half of what was needed for good doctoral programs. Meanwhile Stony Brook built lavish physics labs designed to produce a generation of Nobel Prize winners, which never happened, and one of the most elaborate and expensive medical centers in the world. The faculty at the Stony Brook medical school spent more time in intramural feuds than in trying to achieve research breakthroughs. A medical school dean at Stony Brook had a professional life expectancy of at most three years. And the state of New York did not even need another medical school: it had already two good ones, in Brooklyn and Syracuse.

Unlike Stony Brook, SUNY Binghamton was not created *ab novo* but was built upon a small state liberal arts college, Harpur College, which had existed since 1945. After the war, with lots of people enjoying veterans' benefits of free college education—the G.I. Bill—some local entrepreneurs on the banks of the Susquehanna had the bright idea of creating a liberal arts college to serve this veterans' clientele and other locals of the college-age population. In the postwar depressed academic job market the college administrators had no trouble recruiting respectable Ph.D.s, at least half of them from Robert Maynard Hutchins' University of Chicago, to staff the college.

They chose to name the college after one Robert Harpur, a land speculator of somewhat doubtful reputation, who had played a key role in the early nineteenth century in attracting settlers to the banks of the Susquehanna, the longest unnavigable river in America and strangely a river that had the capacity to stir romantic imaginations. In the early years of the nineteenth century the English poets Robert Southey and Samuel Taylor Coleridge for a short spell had dreamed of establishing a utopian community in Susquehanna country.

By early 1953, as the G.I. Bill students had departed, enrollments fell at little Harpur College, and the college was on the verge of closing down. At this point some local politicians convinced the state of New York to fund Harpur as a state college. In the mid-1960s Harpur was swallowed up into the new expanding SUNY system. But it was not to remain the small liberal arts college devoted to close reading of literary and philosophical texts as the essence of the curriculum, as Robert Maynard Hutchins had propounded at Chicago (amidst enormous controversy that almost broke that university apart). The Republican state senator from Binghamton was also the chairman of the legislative Budget Committee, which made him next to Governor Rockefeller himself the most powerful politician in Albany. This worthy was naturally concerned by IBM's sudden transference of its executive and research personnel downstate, plunging Binghamton into depressed economic conditions.

For Rockefeller to carry out his ambitious plans for creating thirty-two campuses for SUNY, the governor would have to endorse a fourth University Center (doctoral-level school), decreed the senator, besides the other three of Stony Brook, Buffalo, and Albany already planned. Thus, against the wishes of the majority of old Harpur College faculty did this quiet Susquehanna educational homestead become overnight officially the State University of New York at Binghamton. The president and vice president of the campus were not eager to speed the huge expansion and curricular modification this change required. As late as 1974 the sign at the entrance to the campus proclaimed Harpur College and in much smaller letters underneath SUNY-Binghamton. This made the Harpur Chicago Ph.D.s happy as they drove onto the campus—it was still old Harpur College but they generously acquiesced in the much improved salaries and benefits that designation of the campus as a University Center entailed.

The Central Administration in Albany saw that developments at Binghamton were dragging along in slow motion and that the campus was underspending its budget and not filling the generous allotment of new and high-paying faculty lines worthy of a University Center the campus ostensibly had become. Central Administration feared the wrath of the local senator and the governor at this stalling. Instead of removing the lackadaisical president and timid vice president, they saw to it that a bright young economist, Peter Vukasin, was made dean of Arts and Science. With the help of another energetic economist, Robert Melville, as associate dean, Vukasin rapidly laid the foundations of Binghamton as a University Center.

In a half dozen years Vukasin tripled the size of the faculty, bringing in me among the others, and got the Central Administration to undertake an ambitious building program to shape a suitable campus for a quality graduate school. When I first stepped onto the campus in 1970, where I would spend six years, it was most remarkable not for its shabby and small old buildings left over from somnolent Harpur days, but for the mud and dust that accompanied the hasty erection of much larger and in a few instances better looking buildings.

Vukasin was the most energetic, courageous, and far-seeing university administrator I have ever encountered. He made too many enemies from the old Harpur faculty to ever become the president of Binghamton, a position which he richly deserved, and also failed to get the presidency of any other SUNY campus. By 1983 he was retired and living in Massachusetts, a great loss to American higher education, but not the first nor last of academic administrators who failed by succeeding. The pages of the history of American higher education are sprinkled with the names of leaders like Peter Vukasin who were forced to fall on their swords. In the early seventies I idolized Peter Vukasin just as I had Ted Mommsen in the fifties.

In 1970 the Chicago and Harvard Ph.D.s still comprising the majority of the dozen faculty in the Binghamton History Department were willing to accept me as chairman as well as Distinguished Professor because as Donald Kelley, one of them, said in his 1999 review of my book on the common law, I had a reputation, now starting to fade, as the most brilliant young medievalist of my generation. Plus, my publications were somewhat abnormally imaginative and readable exemplars of traditional academic scholarship. I insisted on becoming chairman when Vukasin offered me the Distinguished appointment because the department had an allocation of eleven new faculty lines and I wanted to make sure that the right people were identified and recruited.

Most of my time in the next three years was taken up by the process of faculty recruitment. When I went to the job fair at the American Historical Association meeting at Christmas, I never got out of my hotel room. I spent twelve hours a day for three days interviewing and screening applicants to be invited to the campus. I spent many frustrating hours at the 1930s Flying Jack style Binghamton airport, built on a fog-enshrouded sheared-off Appalachian hill, with no equipment for instrument landing, waiting for a delayed Mohawk Airlines flight to deliver a candidate for his or her campus visit. Locals called it Slohawk Airlines; its president appropriately committed suicide in a fit of despondency. It is now part of U.S. Air, another shambles.

I hired among others one African American, one Latin American Hispanic, and five women. The latter feminist push was due not so much to affirmative action, which I strongly believed in at the time, but because I thought women Ph.D.s were an underutilized pool of high quality. But my three best women appointees soon departed—to Johns Hopkins, Berkeley, and Irvine. I could hire them but I couldn't keep them. They disliked the old Harpur crowd and they found Binghamton an unsuitable ambience for unmarried young women. Feminists complaining that not enough women are hired in universities never factor in this consideration. Still I built up a good department. It wasn't Princeton but it was close to Brandeis in quality and much larger than Brandeis' department with a better library.

One problem I had not foreseen was that there was no local population to include in the pool of graduate students. All the graduate students had to be imported and well paid with fellowships and teaching assistantships to come to this remote area. In the beginning this was easy; there were plenty of student support funds. But with this expenditure for every new entering class of graduate students, by the last year of my chairmanship a tight situation loomed on the horizon. In 1974 I accepted the deanship of the Graduate School partly to deal with this situation by reallocating student aid from lower quality departments. This act, of course, aroused deep resentment, as does any rational act in academic administration.

It was during my six years at Binghamton, four in the History Department, two in the upper echelons of the campus administration, that I saw that the transition from the old academic culture that I had breathed at Princeton and Oxford to the emerging new academic culture that I had absorbed at Columbia and Brandeis, would not be an easy one. Instead, an ideological conflict was developing that continues to the present day. It is called "the culture wars."

Another problem was that the innovative and egalitarian attitudes of the new culture, when transmitted to students, encouraged political activism that I was uncomfortable with and that made the new culture vulnerable to accusations of politicization and lowering of instructional standards. These accusations still linger among holdouts for the old humanist culture and is not without some relationship to reality.

What I liked about the emerging new culture was first of all its blending of the traditional humanities with the social and behavioral sciences in an interdisciplinary fashion, and secondly its recognition of the importance and integrity of popular culture such as television, film, jazz, and rock.

Thirdly, I was temperamentally inclined toward the new culture because it was a form of neo-romanticism. The old culture was rationalistic and objectivist, Aristotelian and aiming to be impersonal. It believed in the power of the human mind to accumulate data whether from written texts, its favorite source, or from controlled experience and inductively derive from this data a structured and fixed truth. It was a world of science, whether in physics or literature.

The new culture was relativist and subjective, Platonic. Truth was not fixed; it was something learned through personal quest and sudden illumination. It was an individual way of looking on the world whose structure was never solid and completed but was always in the course of developing. What we lived by was our personal perception of ideas, not the ideas themselves, which may or may not exist.

In modern times this relativist and neo-romantic view derived from the writings of Karl Marx, Sigmund Freud, and Friedrich Nietzsche and also the American pragmatists William James and John Dewey and the German philosopher Martin Heidegger. In Heidegger's version it was called phenomenology. The new culture believed with the early nineteenth-century romantics that poets and artists are the legislators of mankind, that revelation of truth comes from sensibility, deep feeling, charismatic inspiration, rather than from organized pursuit of data collection and systematic reasoning. It believed in the charismatic thinker, the seer who saw truth and heard messages.

I liked these assumptions of the new culture. I could not resist them. They were one with what I had always viscerally believed. At the same time, however, I disliked and feared the leftist activism that was attached to the new culture, not so much from the students as among the faculty. The new generation of leftist professors emerging from graduate schools in the 1970s, I found uncivil, dogmatic, and unreliable. They looked upon me as a redundant fossil of the old culture playing an untrustworthy and manipulative game by mouthing sympathy for fragments of the new culture.

I stood between a dying cultural world and one struggling to be born, and I would be consumed by angry legions on both sides. My vulnerable and ambiguous placement in the cultural wars of the 1970s and 1980s contributed to my dramatic and repeated failures as a high-level university administrator.

The old culture was a creation of white males, some still living, most of them dead, an upper middle-class "episteme" (thought-world). The new culture worshiped at the shrine of women goddesses and enjoyed the taste of the unfamiliar societies and their people of color.

The new culture was on a voyage of discovery. For the old culture, the great discoveries had been made long ago, in some quasi-mythical past, and had to be retained now to foster group identity and generational transference.

The old culture was dominated by the printed word in set texts. The new culture believed that surface meanings elucidated from the text had no special legitimacy. The truth lay in subordinate levels of meaning below the surface of the text or in some social or psychic illumination imposed on the text from the outside.

What distinguished the new culture from the old was the matter of boundaries between disciplines. The old culture believed that history, literature, and philosophy were distinct disciplines, discrete intellectual codes. Of course it was noticed that at the margin there was some overlapping of the disciplines. But this was an unpursued accident.

The new culture did not want to live behind closed doors. Everything was thrown open. The strictness of boundaries was changed into a conscious effort to foster interdisciplinary and multidisciplinary inquiries, to blend rather than separate. Calm and cultivation were to be replaced by innovation and outrage. All media were legitimate.

A distinction between the old and new cultures was the former's objectivity and permanence against the latter's subjectivity and transience. The old culture was slow and careful about announcing that the truth had been realized, but if it had been sustained through enduring scientific analysis then the truth was firmly embraced.

The new culture was wary of declaring anything true in a scientific and rational sense. It was pragmatic and phenomenological. The latter term means the new culture felt we could experience expression and affect and notice their impact, but we could never break through to objectivity and finitude.

This idea was as old as Immanuel Kant's *Critique of Pure Reason* (1790) or perhaps William of Occam around 1310. But the new culture marketed this idea in dazzling ways.

The old culture was centrist liberal or moderately conservative politically. The new culture tried to avoid such limitations and determination. It said: X is what we know but we only see one side of it. The truth resides on the other side of the planet—the truth is out there, somewhere. If we find it, it will surprise us. Probably we will never find it.

Assuredly the great majority of college students and graduate students never understood this clear antinomy between the two cultures. Frustrated journalists could not articulate the differences although they sensationalized whatever fragments they could identify. The war between the old and new cultures was a conflict within the faculty and their immediate followers among the brighter doctoral students.

By 1990 positions had hardened, polemics were elaborated. The two sides stopped listening to one another. A number of faculty withdrew from the intellectual turmoil and chose comfortable ambiences and descended into affluent and privileged privatism. Social responsibility and intellectual regard were mitigated. Power centers and brokers cut off debate. Refined intellectual discourse descended into sloganeering and blood feuds.

Along with the fiscal problems of the universities I was involved with from 1960 to 1976—Columbia, Brandeis, and Binghamton—were the tides of the campus leftist activism. Fostered by generational rebellion against the bleakness of new suburbia, by the moral earnestness generated by the Cold War, and the runaway prosperity of the 1960s which guaranteed every college graduate a job and wiped away the cautionary reticence induced by the Great Depression of the 1930s, each of these three campuses along with many others in America became flashpoints of student and faculty activism.

The civil rights movement, the tensions of bringing African Americans onto the mainstream campuses for the first time in significant numbers, and the hysteria generated by the military draft for the Vietnam War drove the igniting of radical behavior.

The radical campus movement of the late 1960s and early 1970s signified the incapacity of the old academic culture to confront and control social and cultural change. Columbia College had, next to the University of Chicago, the most intensive drilling for undergraduates in the philosophical and literary canon as it was now called—the set texts of Western Civilization—of any campus in the country. All that reading of Plato, Aquinas, Dante, and Locke did not mollify the noisy minority of activist students who claimed that the University was an arm of the industrial and military complex and racist because it wanted to build a gymnasium in Morningside Park that separated the campus from Harlem.

Nor did all the tweedy seminars for graduate students in the best humanities programs dissuade a large segment of the new Ph.D.s that started teaching after 1965 from assuming fierce radical postures. In the latter regard, I think especially of the Yale History Department in the 1960s and 1970s when its luminary in American history, the slightly left of center liberal southerner C. Vann Woodward, turned out dozens of well-trained Ph.D.s among whom were a remarkable number of the radicals of the new generation of academics.

I surmise that close biographical study of Vann Woodward's army of Ph.D.s would show that their leftist ideology stemmed from their family and class backgrounds rather than from Woodward's teaching. Woodward, however, tolerated their radicalism and made their academic careers possible and gave them the professional training to insert their ideology into their research.

Did the Ivy League liberals ever consider the consequence of unleashing their obviously radical Ph.D.s onto the U.S. campuses? In the interests of academic freedom, apparently not. The old culture was too soft and porous and perhaps lazy to confront the political situation.

I had left Columbia by two years when the events of May 1968 occurred there: the occupation for two weeks of five buildings including the president's office by student radicals, their eviction by a nighttime police action mandated by President Dwight Eisenhower's pompous and unwise successor, Grayson Kirk. The commotion and media frenzy brought down not only the immobile Kirk but also the new provost, David Truman, a faculty leader whom I greatly admired. Truman ended up not as president of Columbia for which he was destined, but saving pieces of his shattered career, as president of Mount Holyoke College for Women.

As president of Brandeis, Morris Abrams confronted the takeover of the modest campus computer center by a dozen African American students. He magnified this jejune and harmless incident into a national event, reliving his glory days as a civil rights lawyer in segregated Georgia. He called in the TV networks; he wrote an inflammatory article for the *New York Times Magazine*. He summoned faculty to an emergency meeting at the same time as the Super Bowl was being played. The Trustees were infuriated. They knew that the overwhelming majority of middle-class Jewish parents were entirely unsympathetic to the African American dissidents. They showed Abrams the door in a hasty and cruel manner. Isolated Binghamton up at the confluence of the Catskills and Appalachians took a long time to imitate these events. It was not until 1977 that a small group of African American students and their allies took over the administration building for a couple of days, to no consequence whatsoever.

Two of the leaders of the Columbia Revolution were my students and I had, they claimed, inspired them by my neo-romantic teaching and my frequent sarcastic reference to the failings of Grayson Kirk and his administration. The leader of the tepid little Binghamton imbroglio was my own doctoral student. He is now head of the African American Studies program at conservative Boston University and is as respectable as they come.

I empathized with the student activists but I never did anything to help them. It was the faculty radicals who gave me pause. I never thought that student demonstrations and building takeovers were more than game playing. But the new generation of faculty radicals had something serious in mind. They wanted not only good campus jobs for themselves, which they normally deserved, but also the exercise of power in higher education.

First they would get it by stimulating students to political action. Then in time they would control departments, select new faculty, and distribute graduate student aid on grounds of ideology, race, and gender. In time they would emerge in the higher levels of administration and in control of institutes and thereby command the patronage to induce obedience to themselves as campus commissars.

I witnessed all this beginning to happen in the 1970s and never perceived a way to stop it. It was a movement, a rolling tide, a cultural transformation. Whenever I questioned the leftist advance in academia, I was denounced as a fool and a reactionary. But the more conservative faculty still committed to British humanism also did not trust me. They saw me as a Trojan Horse for the radical takeover, as untrustworthy and dangerous. They were not wrong, because I had mixed feelings about the leftist advance. I agreed with many of its ideas and attitudes and I was in no temperamental condition to fight it. I was caught between two polarized worlds.

By the spring of 1967 I had to admit to myself that I had made a terrible mistake in going to Brandeis. The situation there was hopeless and would never improve. I cut my teaching back to the legal minimum; I was on campus not more than eight hours a week.

In the top floor of my house in Lexington I created a study for myself. I installed a state-of-the-art stereo system designed to play classical records for five hours nonstop. I turned to writing. Like so much I have done in my life I achieved early success and then miserable failure.

Together with a former Columbia student of mine, Richard I. Schneider of York University in Toronto, I wrote a short handbook for history majors, *How to Study History*. Richard wrote one and a half of the five chapters, but with my characteristic sloppiness in money matters I let him have half the royalties, which he shrewdly invested in the booming Toronto real estate market and became affluent.

How to Study History is still in print four decades later; it has gone through forty printings with two different publishers. It is emblematic of the old humanist culture. There is very little of the new culture in it. I felt that was where the market then lay. If I wrote it today, it would be a different book.

My second effort, which was mostly written while I was still at Columbia but finished in Lexington, the stereo churning away, was *The English*, a political and social history of England to 1760. Through Leonard Levy's literary agent the book was sold to Michael Korda at Simon and Schuster. Korda, who had been raised and educated in England, said this was the book that he had always been looking for in prep school and college. Someone had finally made sense out of English history. He took my wife and me to lunch near Rockefeller Center and predicted big things of the book.

It was not to be, mainly due to a devastating review in *The New York Review of Books* by Princeton's Lawrence Stone. He had requested the book for review from his pal, the *Review's* editor, Robert Silvers, who had made his weekly into an arbiter of academic ideas.

My book was essentially a liberal or "Whiggish" approach glossed over with a thin layer of romantic sentimentality. Stone contemptuously stripped away this layer and trashed the book as old-fashioned, out-of-date reactionary British humanism. Stone turned a historical debate into an ideological war and a personal blood feud. Stone was a product of that 1940s British academic generation who had completely lost faith in the English liberal tradition under whose aegis Britain had become a humane, rich, and powerful country. He was a Marxist and a Nihilist.

I have always thought that the vicious tone of Stone's review was meant to drive a stake through the heart of Joe Strayer, still teaching at

Princeton. It was intended to tell Strayer that his era in the Princeton History Department was over; the Stone era had begun. What better way to proclaim this than to trash a book written by Strayer's student and sometime protégé?

Shortly after the book appeared in 1968 I had a long interview with Robert Lopez, the medievalist at Yale. He told me that Strayer had said very good things about the book to him. I had that small satisfaction.

The paperback rights to *The English* were about to be bought by Penguin in Britain—who agreed with Korda's enthusiastic assessment—for a big advance. Stone's assault finished that possibility. Stone took food out of my children's mouths. He was Satan in my eyes.

The third publishing venture, and second failure, was less shriekingly painful but even more costly to me in time and money. I accepted a remarkable offer from Scott Foresman, a major textbook publisher, in Chicago to write a new two-volume history of Western Civilization. The company executive who approached me in the fall of 1966 was David Halphen, a well spoken, insightful, pleasant man—not your normal thuggish textbook editor—who had taken a doctorate in French literature after the War at the Sorbonne on the G.I. Bill.

Halphen felt that the two or three Western Civilization textbooks dominating the freshman field were tired and out of date. He thought I could take a fresh approach and we met several times in Glenwood, Illinois, the suburban Chicago home of Scott Foresman, to thrash out the details of a bold plan I presented. The publisher poured $150,000 in 1999 dollars into my preparation of the manuscript. Of that I took only $15,000 for myself. With the rest of the money I hired four young research assistants, two from Harvard, and a full-time secretary, a highly literate and sharp Bryn Mawr graduate, and to my wife's distaste I set up an atelier on the top floor of our three-floor house in Lexington. I finished the basement and turned it into a game room with a dartboard, a ping pong table, a billiard table, and a large TV. It was like the early days of Apple under Steve Jobs. Unfortunately the results were not Macintosh but a sour apple—a textbook that commercially failed, at least according to Scott Foresman's high expectations.

I envisioned a three-track, two-volume book, blending the old and new academic cultures. The first track was environmental and material history, "the New Social History" as it was euphemistically called. The third track was lavishly illustrated cultural history in which the color pictures told much of the story—British humanism visually presented. The middle track was conventional political and economic history but told pithily in simple language.

This is where a problem lay. Nervous at such an innovative design, Halphen set up a panel of old culture academics at leading universities to review each chapter as my Bryn Mawr secretary and an Italian working-class backup typist put the text through their clacking IBM Selectrics. The black and white pictures for track one, the material environment, and the color pictures for track three, the cultural history, would be added later in that pre-computer era, painfully pasted onto the page.

The academic critics had little or nothing to say about the fragmentary tracks one and three, which because of their visual incompleteness were hard to imagine as finished work. The academic experts concentrated on the much more conventional track two, political and economic narrative, in which they in any case felt at home. They complained loudly about the succinctness and brevity of the conventional narrative ("How can Cantor devote only four pages to the Thirty Years

War?") and wanting also to earn their reviewer's fees, proposed a multitude of additions. The book swelled and in the end the two-volume work came out at fourteen hundred pages.

I still marvel that even with my gang of assistants I could have produced this bloated monstrosity in just under three years of work. I told Halphen to fire the academic critics and let me go it alone. He was too nervous about the new culture components in the book to do that. I told him the book was at least one-third too long for students in community and lower echelon four year colleges, our prime market. He insisted that I push on. He thought of himself grandiosely as the producer of a work that would revolutionize college Western Civilization education.

I did not tell him that the biggest problem with my book was that it was too sophisticated for 80 percent of college teachers in Western Civilization courses. They would be afraid to give the book to their students because the students would then raise questions and want to pursue theories that were beyond the capacity and learning of the instructors.

By 1972, when I was already deep into my chairmanship at Binghamton, the book had sold enough copies that Scott Foresman had made back its sizable investment. Then the company faced the problem of declining sales because of the used book market. Halphen's hope that the book was so interesting and well illustrated that students would not sell it back to college bookstores at the end of the course proved vain. Halphen flew out from Chicago and told me that Scott Foresman was letting the book go out of print. Then he took a $10,000 company check from his pocket and gave it to me as a farewell present. I wondered how big a fight he had at Scott Foresman to get his bosses to make this gesture.

I had made a great effort to recast myself as a textbook writer. I had failed.

Combined with my marginalization as a teacher, I saw my academic career in shambles and I responded to an opportunity to enter the higher levels of university administration at Binghamton and establish a new career. From that putatively elevated vantage point, I could do something to reward good teaching and effect the blending of the old and new academic cultures.

Once again I was naïve and uninformed when I entered university administration. I neither realized the only marginal impact that administrators could exercise on the content and actual delivery of academic programs, nor did I anticipate the power struggles, personality clashes, and mischievous turf-building that occurred grotesquely at the upper administrative level.

❖ 5 ❖

LEADERSHIP AND POWER

In the thirty-five years before 1965 high-level university adminis-trators—president, provost (academic vice president) and dean of a school—were characteristically low-key and quiet people. The first age of expansion of American universities, when bold vision and high energy were admired qualities, covered the first three decades of the twentieth century. With the onset of the Great Depression of the 1930s retrenchment, parsimony, and caution became the watchwords of university administrators. A conservative, almost immobile attitude, was further conditioned by the military draft from 1940 to 1945 which again drastically shrank the student body.

There was a reversal in the six or seven years after the War when Johnny came marching home again and was able to attend college under the G.I. Bill, allowing entry to higher education of economic and ethnic groups who hitherto had been all but excluded from campuses. But the university administrators were still cautious about expansion both of the faculty and of the campus infrastructure.

Tenure track faculty lines increased only slightly (much use was made of temporary and part-time instructors) and instead of permanent new buildings for classrooms and dormitories, short-lived wooden structures such as had previously dotted the country in army camps were now erected on campuses. By 1952 university administrators could feel satisfied with their cautious response to the challenge of the post-war G.I. Bill. The veterans left, the size of freshman classes diminished, and the reintroduction of the draft during the Korean War indicated that it was better to be safe than sorry about university expansion.

The sole visionary and activist among university presidents during the thirties and forties, Robert Maynard Hutchins at the University of Chicago, with his according of priority to undergraduate education and a core classical curriculum, finally departed to head a foundation, to the relief of the majority of the faculty. Nicholas Murray Butler, who had taken Columbia to world-class level, passed first into his dotage and then into his grave. He was succeeded by indifferent or incompetent men.

General Dwight Eisenhower became president of Columbia from 1948 to 1952 because New York liberal Republicans, who dominated the university's Board of Trustees, needed a place to park the great soldier until the 1952 presidential election campaign came around. The presidency of a major university was the ideal job for Ike: he had a good salary, excellent benefits, a beautiful house, favorable treatment in the media, and he had to do nothing as Columbia's president. He ran his executive staff meetings as though he were again preparing to invade Normandy, except that D-day never came. An obscure political scientist named Grayson Kirk became Eisenhower's *aide-de-camp* and shuffled papers for him. Kirk succeeded to the Columbia presidency after Eisenhower and lasted until the upheavals of 1968, slowly guiding the world's greatest university into penury and somnolence.

The most admired and most emulated university president of the postwar era was Harvard's James B. Conant. He was a chemist chosen in secret by the Harvard Trustees without consulting the faculty. In WWI Conant spent his time perfecting poison gas. In WWII he worked on the atom bomb project. After Harvard, he was High Commissioner to Germany and played an important role in the Cold War and the building of the Federal Republic of Germany. It could be said that Conant made three important decisions that shaped postwar America and that they were all the wrong ones. Unlike most scientists, he strongly favored Hiroshima. He forgave the many surviving Nazis in the interests of the Cold War. And he decided that tenure at Harvard should be based on research and publication; teaching would take care of itself.

Conant personified the tough guy public culture of postwar America and the rise of the federally supported research university. He also played a key role in the organization of the National Science Foundation, whose grants would be decided by peer review—actually fear review, the senior scientists deciding which of the junior ones to support. Conant, however, turned out to be a first-rate, hands-on, day-to-day administrator.

After Conant, the Harvard Trustees went for a mystic and theologian, Nathan Pusey, a Harvard alumnus who was vegetating as the prexy of a small college in Wisconsin. Pusey had no interest in day-to-day administration nor in the university programs except for the tiny Divinity School. He was a devout Christian, something of a mystic, and he greatly expanded the Divinity School, making some good faculty appointments therein. He left the actual running of Harvard to the deans of each faculty.

This gave McGeorge Bundy, a precocious political scientist and Boston Brahmin, the opportunity as dean of the Faculty of Arts and Science to exercise very strong leadership, expand the faculty, and set very high standards for tenure. Research productivity and national academic visibility were now the requirements for tenure at Harvard. It was assumed, wrongly of course, that good undergraduate teaching automatically accompanied these other allegedly rarer qualities.

By 1960 half of the teaching in the Harvard undergraduate college was being done not by full-time faculty but by graduate student teaching assistants. The latter, while hard pressed to finish up their doctorates, were uniformly of the highest quality intellectually; what they did in the classroom naturally varied.

Presidents and deans in the fifty leading universities envied McGeorge Bundy and, so far as their usually more modest resources allowed, emulated him. He was the tall shadow in American higher education in the fifties and sixties until he left to become one of Lyndon Johnson's chief advisors on Vietnam and thereby damaged his golden academic reputation. But then Bundy took over as president of the Ford Foundation, the richest in the world, and removed some of his Vietnam tarnish by directing Ford in a leftist direction, giving priority to Third World causes abroad and African American needs at home.

McGeorge Bundy was a handsome, energetic, shrewd, and courageous man, undoubtedly one of the great figures in American higher education. He was a superb public speaker and a very good writer and scholar as he proved, when in the 1980s as a professor at NYU, he produced a prizewinning history of American nuclear policy.

But the kind of elitist world Bundy dealt with at Harvard, while a good model for Princeton and Yale, was irrelevant to almost every other institution in American education. The problem by the 1960s was not how to achieve higher quality in an already superior, stable, and well-funded campus. It was rather how to deal with the tidal wave of students from the postwar, baby boom generation heading for campuses of all kinds; how to identify, recruit, and socialize the legion of new Ph.D.s needed to contend with the demographic tidal wave; how to supervise the rapid physical expansion of campuses or plan new ones so that they became environments amenable for undergraduates and graduates. This was not Bundy-land.

Various presidents and chancellors, legions of provosts and deans led by Chancellor Clark Kerr in the University of California's nine campus system were viewed as doing the best job of monitoring and channeling the massive expansion, until the student revolution began on the Berkeley campus in 1964. Its leader, Mario Savio, a graduate student—and later college instructor—in mathematics, denounced Berkeley and the California system as a soulless, harsh megalopolis tied to capitalist oligarchy and the Department of Defense. Perhaps after all, California didn't have all the answers, but then nobody did.

The essential problem of the expansionary era from 1958 to 1974 was that university administrators had spent so many decades following a policy of stasis, moderation, and retrenchment that they did not know how to plan for and deal with the challenge of physical expansion, social democratization of the student body, curricular innovation, and cultural change. How would McGeorge Bundy have done as president at Stony Brook or Binghamton, exemplars of the frontline action of the 1960s and early 1970s? No one knows; of course he would never have accepted the job on the raw, frenetic new campuses.

The president of Binghamton who offered me the deanship of the Graduate School in 1974 was Clifford Clark. He was a laconic, witty, learned, sensitive economist from the Midwest who had come to Binghamton shortly after I did to become dean of the Business School. He was not your ordinary aggressive business school dean, but on the downside, he was deficient in the hard-driving entrepreneurial qualities of a business school dean. I had campaigned for his elevation to the presidency, turning my back on Peter Vukasin, who I figured had no chance because of the hostility of the old Harpur College crowd toward him.

Clark saw immediately that he had a severe problem with the Graduate School, which I was appointed to fix. It had no less than thirteen doctoral programs, but many had developed in such a slovenly manner and were in the hands of such mediocre faculty that they would not survive close scrutiny from the SUNY Central Administration nor the State Commissioner of Higher Education. The worst example was the Physics Department. There a group of unknown and unproductive scientists tried to run a graduate program with homemade research equipment they had manufactured themselves because they lacked research grants. It was something out of a Dickens novel or a Rube Goldberg cartoon.

The English Department had some excellent faculty but also some very weak ones. It was not careful in its recruitment of younger faculty; it was stocking up on more of the Hutchins classical fanatics. It accepted and funded just about any graduate student who applied, some of whom became activist troublemakers. The English doctoral program had to be pruned and trimmed and its mission clearly defined. The Mathematics Department was immobilized by a civil war among its faculty over some arcane disciplinary theories. And so forth.

Clark gave me *carte blanche* to clean out the Augean Stables. And I did so. After first spending a few days in Albany gauging the mind-set of the Central Administration officials—surprisingly progressive and cooperative people—and that of the State Education Department (menacing and mischievous) who together determined the campus budget, I undertook a zero base budget analysis of each department's graduate program, discovering where every dollar went and requiring a department to justify each budget line in terms of performance and productivity.

I derived this method from Robert McNamara's reform of the Pentagon after he had done the same things at Ford Motor Company. It was called PPB—program planning budgeting. Totally unfamiliar on the Binghamton campus, it aroused deep resentment in many quarters, especially when the following year having been promoted by Clark to Vice Chancellor for Academic Affairs, I applied PPB to the campus as a whole. As a business school dean, Clark appreciated what I was doing, although from the beginning, with an acute political sense, he worried about its ramifications in terms of faculty-administration relationships.

The civil servants in Albany were delighted. For once they received a campus annual budget proposal that was readable, accurate, and informative. At this time the colleges of the City University of New York had come on the state education budget for the first time. The administrators on the CUNY campuses had no idea what a program budget looked like—previously on New York City funding, they had followed the rules of Tammany Hall, not the Pentagon. When the provost at City College in Manhattan phoned the state budget director for higher education in Albany for advice, she was told to get a copy of Cantor's Binghamton budget and do the same thing. That must have sent a shock through the disorganized old campus on Broadway and 137th Street.

I discovered as Binghamton provost that the great majority of deans and department chairs were not interested in a budgetary system in which funds were allocated rationally on an annual basis in accordance with programmatic needs and proven performance. It was hard to get chairs to even read their annual budgets. The faculty mind-set, prevalent among department chairs and even many deans, favored operation on a political system, not a budgetary one.

They wanted to drop in on the provost and make a personal pitch for funding at any time of the year. What appalled me was that many upper level administrators (presidents, provosts, and deans) as well as departmental chairs and faculty liked this political system. It was what I called the Tammany Hall version of university administration—allocation by cronyism and handing out of personal largesse from the boss.

If the good years under Rockefeller had continued under the new governor, Hugh Carey, I would have been very successful as provost at Binghamton. But instead Carey imposed a 5 percent retrenchment on the SUNY budget for 1976. Clark put me in charge of responding to this mandate. I established a twenty-five-person faculty and student committee. We worked for two weeks in July and easily met our goals.

Four doctoral programs, including that of the barefoot mountain boys in the Physics Department, were eliminated. The English Department lost two junior faculty lines which they in no way needed—how many Tennyson or even Chaucer experts does a campus need? The one-person Russian Department personified by an elderly gentleman right out of Tsarist Russia was cut; there were one or two local people who could teach basic Russian better, although not Tolstoy. Some useless administrative officers were eliminated. The campus looked *better*, not worse, after these cutbacks.

But led by the corpulent, scheming chairman of the English Department and an obscure mathematician who was head of the faculty union, there was an explosion on campus. An emergency meeting of the faculty condemned me. I submitted my resignation to Clark; he refused to accept it. I came back and carried out my plan, which was praised in Albany.

But my legitimacy had been damaged and it was clear that Clark was nervous about keeping me on. He was an expert in business management but when the Binghamton faculty, like nearly all faculty elsewhere, rebelled against a managerial approach to campus budgeting, he switched to conceding the utility of the political model in which an English Department chair and a faculty union hack could shred the most careful kind of program performance analysis and review of unit needs.

The faculty's view must be seen in context. They had witnessed a steady expansion of academic unit budgets and an increase in their salaries and budgets since around 1964 without feeling any pressure to increase their own productivity. They did not want to hear that this era of expansion was drawing to a close. Any high level administrator who told them that seemed malevolent and had to be removed.

I responded to ads for provosts in the *Chronicle of Higher Education*, and on the July 4th weekend of 1976, I was offered the same position as I held at Binghamton at the University of Illinois-Chicago Circle, a new urban state campus twice the size of Binghamton in the number of faculty and students. With no enthusiasm on the part of my wife and daughter (my son was headed to college and didn't care), I sacrificed the splendid house on a hill in Binghamton in a very depressed real estate market and moved to Chicago at the end of August 1976. My wife found a small apartment for us on Lakeshore Drive.

Illinois-Chicago Circle, after joining with the then separate University Medical Center located a mile away, is now called simply Illinois-Chicago. I liked the name Chicago Circle because it allowed me to say that the campus had something in common with Oxford, which was also named after a traffic device—"Oxenaford," the original Old English word, meant a "ford for oxen." Chicago Circle was built from the ground up in the late 1960s at the junction of the two big state freeway systems in downtown Chicago, a couple of miles west of the business district and the lakefront.

It was Mayor Richard Daley's university. He wanted a large urban campus to serve the needs of both his middle-class and his working-class constituents. The old land grant institution in Urbana-Champaign was opposed. But Daley said to make his university a U.I. campus or he would tell the Governor and legislature that we would go it alone and charter an independent campus, which would directly compete with old Urbana for state funding. Unfortunately for the future of Chicago Circle, and me, the good old boys in Urbana caved in and gave Daley his ill-fated and grossly underfunded campus.

They figured that by bringing Circle under their supervision as a U.I. campus, they could limit its budget and not diminish the lavish funding that Urbana received from the state. Just as important, the president of the new three campus system—Urbana, Circle, and the then separate Medical Center—would tightly control the Illinois Foundation, an extremely prosperous conduit for fundraising in the private sector, further limiting Circle's income. Daley did not see these pitfalls. Happy to get his campus anointed with the charisma of the University of Illinois' venerable name, he made the wrong decision with regard to Circle's status.

An area peopled by the Greek and Italian voters who were paradoxically among Daley's strongest supporters was leveled and a huge complex of buildings was erected over a two-year period. It cost $100 million in 1970 dollars ($300 million today) and was one of the most ambitious university building projects in American history. The campus was designed by Walter Netsch of Skidmore, Owings, and Merrill, Chicago's premiere architectural firm.

The campus resembled a moon station in some galactic future—huge concrete buildings and two levels of walkways between them. The first winter the campus was open it was discovered that the upper-level walkway got covered with ice and was unusable for five months a year.

Netsch had all sorts of idiosyncratic ideas, including a pseudo-classical amphitheater in the open air, for which also little use was found. The engineering building featured three-story high laboratories that seemed ready to house rocket ships. It was in fact here that the computer graphics first used extensively in *Star Wars* were developed by a young assistant professor. Another young member of the engineering faculty for a year was later infamous as the Unabomber.

Netsch, who seems to have not been on a campus since his own college days, forgot about the importance of a library. All his buildings were grotesquely overdone, but the library was so tiny it would have disgraced a community college. The student center was, however, right on the mark for an urban commuter campus—excellent dining facilities, many lounges, a bowling alley, and a much used film theater.

Two weeks after Labor Day 1976, the first day of classes found me on the twenty-seventh floor of Circle's twenty-eight-floor Administration and Liberal Arts building ensconced in a large and expensively furnished office, surrounded by no less than three secretaries, two associate vice chancellors, and an administrative assistant. Like the Big Ten universities in general, the University of Illinois believed in heavy administrative staffing by a hoary formula devised around 1925. I had no use for the administrative assistant, an upper-class suburbanite. When I tried to get rid of her, I discovered that (like many of the administrative staff—this was Chicago after all) she had political connections. I arranged for a subsidized, six-month internship for her in a federal agency in D.C. "for further training." Shortly after her return to Chicago, to my surprise, she became a dean of some sort at Northwestern!

I loved the secretarial staff. They were all working-class, blue jeans-wearing young women, bright, and high speed at their IBM machines. And I had a lot of memos and letters to write. I was in charge of 1,200 faculty and 20,000 students.

The chancellor, Donald Riddle, had come in the year before I did from the presidency of John Jay College of Criminal Justice in New York City. He was an easy-going, politically savvy executive. Shortly after I began working there, he seems to have secretly suffered a mild stroke. After that he arrived at his aerie duplex office—something out of a Batman film—at 10:00 A.M. and after a long lunch in his office, he left around 3:00 P.M. for his beautiful condo on the lakefront. Riddle left the running of the campus to me and took as his job relations with the system president's office in Urbana, the Governor's Office in Springfield, and money-raising in Chicago. As far as I could see, nothing useful for the Circle campus came out of these responsibilities.

Riddle had done a very good job at John Jay. He treated the Circle chancellorship as much as he could as a sinecure until his retirement. In any case he had been hired as a figurehead to bring peace to the campus and in doing that, he did enough.

The previous and first president of the campus, an engineering dean from Minneapolis, had gotten into a terrible wrangle, about what I never understood, with the very powerful Faculty Council and its chairman, an Education School professor (and later dean), Maurice Eash, and the Council had in effect persuaded the President in Urbana to remove the Chancellor.

The Faculty Council headed by Eash then in succeeding years chose Riddle as chancellor and me as academic vice chancellor. Maurice Eash was a brilliant, hard-working, devout man from a farming community in Indiana who had worked his way up via a doctorate at Columbia Teachers College to national prominence in the field of school operations research. He held and fulfilled innumerable research grants from federal agencies and private foundations. I learned a lot about administration from him and also from another leader of the Faculty Council, the chair of the Geology Department, Werner Baur. He was a German and still had close ties to German universities. Baur was an internationally renowned scientist; he did not take fools, laggards, and amateurs lightly.

The quality of the faculty at Circle was intrinsically as good as at any of the newer public universities. In putting the faculty together in the late 1960s and early 1970s, one big mistake had been made. Care had not been taken to make sure that the professors hired were in fact people who liked to live in cities and were attuned to the problems of urban society. At least two-thirds of the faculty lived in North Shore suburbs. They commuted in by car on the freeway (there were huge cheap parking lots on campus), taught their classes and unless they were running a large laboratory, were on the freeway home by 2:00 P.M.

The undergraduates were in nearly all cases of lower middle class and working class backgrounds. Twenty-five percent were African American and 15 percent were Latino (Latin American Hispanic). Whatever their race or color, they needed a lot of personal attention from the faculty, a lot of mentoring. They got almost none of that. The faculty, with very few exceptions, treated the students as if they came from affluent and literate families, which was rarely the case. An undertow of resentment ran through the student body, especially the 40 percent who were minorities. At least a third of the students were Polish-American working class. Ambitious and hard working, they chafed at anything that seemed to provide special treatment or consideration for Black and Latino minorities. The distant rumble of potential racial conflict could always be heard from the campus high-rise buildings.

I worked night and day from 6:30 A.M. to 7:00 P.M. five days a week and often for six hours on Saturday to overcome these problems among the faculty and students with only marginal progress. I got the funding from Urbana for a social center for the Latino students (the African Americans already had one). I established the PPB zero based budgeting system for the campus, much to the dislike of the lackadaisical Arts and Science dean. I established a Resource and Performance profile for each campus unit to see where the money was going and how it might be better used. With a large faculty committee I held public hearings on the budget of each campus academic unit. The faculty liked this: the deans did not; it put them on the spot. It allowed faculty to see where privileged patronage was going and forced the deans to justify these allocations.

I organized a Research and Contracts Office to foster funded research and greatly expanded grants activity. Looking back in 1999 to 1977, Maurice Eash said that I "established within the faculty a sense of vision of what a Research I urban university could be."

I dealt with a problem that Circle had endured from its opening day. Classes began at 8:00 A.M. and were very heavily enrolled at that hour. The students nearly all held jobs in the Loop or elsewhere in the city. They wanted to get their classes over with, grab a quick lunch in the student center, and go to work by 1:00 P.M. By 2:00 P.M. the campus was almost deserted. Not even the free showing of recently released films at the student center could hold them. What should be done with this vast concrete facility in the afternoon and early evening? An "Extended Day" program was long talked about.

With the help of Maurice Eash and my two associate provosts, Robert Hess (later president of Brooklyn College) and Richard Johnson, I got the Extended Day program moving within a year of my coming to the campus. It was a huge success and marked a new era for Circle. Mature adult students poured consistently onto the campus to get a U.I. degree cheaply. I taught a freshman history survey for a whole semester to seventy-five students at 6:00 P.M. to set an example to the faculty. This was a mistake on my part. It exhausted me so much that I had trouble focusing on my administrative work. Chancellor Riddle warned me, but I did not listen.

I stood at my high office windows on the twenty-seventh floor and watched twenty thousand students pouring onto the campus at 7:45 A.M. How could I help these worthy young people? How could I make their lives better? After the first campus budgetary exercise, by the fall of 1977, I knew that the most important thing I could do was increase the campus budget. Circle was being severely shortchanged by the U.I.

system's President's office in Urbana. I compared Urbana's state budget with Circle and saw that in most programs Circle was underfunded. And beyond the state budget, the Urbana graduate programs were generously subsidized by private funds allocated through the University of Illinois Foundation, which the system President also controlled. Circle saw little of this backdoor private money.

The most obvious difference between Urbana and Circle was in the library. Circle needed a big new library building and a huge boost in its book collection budget. Circle students had little room to work in the current nook that the forgetful architect had provided and these were students who probably did not have a room of their own at home. Graduate students could not make headway through Circle's meager book and journal resources. A device had been worked out allowing Circle students to borrow books from the Urbana Library—which had the third largest university collection in the country—and have the books shipped by truck to Chicago. That was better than nothing. But I tried it out and found it cumbersome and frustrating.

I went to see Riddle and requested permission to talk to the system Vice President for Finance, Ron Brady, the President's protégé, who maintained an office on the Circle campus and was there one day a week. Riddle allowed me to confront Brady but told me not to expect much. For the most part I got nothing. But Brady, an arrogant and bumptious young man, said he would study the library situation for possible entry as a capital budget item to put up a new building.

Months went by. I went to many meetings in Urbana, accompanied by Bob Hess (nephew of the oil magnate) and presented my case over and over again on the library and other budgetary matters. I had a private conference with the system president, John Corbally, a smooth academic politician, later head of the MacArthur Foundation, which putatively chose and funded "geniuses." Corbally had as much capacity to identify geniuses as a deaf mute to select the string section of the Chicago Symphony.

Corbally was a tall heavyset Midwesterner with the face of an Iowa farmer. Put a pair of overalls on him and a pitchfork in his hand and he would be ready to pose for Grant Wood. He had taken a doctorate in education administration at Berkeley and had spent his whole career as a campus bureaucrat, mainly at Ohio State before Urbana.

Corbally's strength was his handling of the Board of Trustees, political hacks elected on the party tickets. They served without pay, but at their monthly meetings Corbally lavished the Trustees with expensive dinners, gifts, and front row tickets to musical comedies. He knew the low intellectual level and poor taste of the Trustees because they were his own. In our brief conference, Corbally would do nothing to overrule Vice President Brady, his pal and hatchet man. I could feel his anti-Semitic contempt for me.

My meetings with Brady and his fiscal staff got more and more heated. Hess started to call me "Stormin' Norman." In one session Brady told me to shut up; he was tired of listening to my harangues. I got up and left the meeting. I walked around the beautiful, immaculate Urbana campus and borrowed from the university library the English translation of a classic work on early medieval society by Georges Duby that had been published two years previously but which I had had no time or inclination in the midst of power struggles to read. I sat in the sunshine, the football band practicing a couple of blocks away, and read

Duby's *Early Growth of the European Economy* for the next two hours until Hess found me and we drove back in silence to Chicago.

Shortly thereafter Riddle came down to my office and told me the good news. Yes, Corbally and the Trustees had agreed to $10 million for a new library for Circle in the U.I. capital budget. It was going before the Board of Trustees at their meeting in Springfield tomorrow; it was all decided: there was no need for me to waste time attending the Trustees meeting—which by state law was open to the public; congratulations, Norman; this is really great, Norman.

The next day, after my lecture in the Extended Day program, I was going home on the bus at 8:00 P.M. I had a copy of the afternoon edition of the *Chicago Tribune*. In the lower corner on the front page was a headline "U.I. Trustees Endorse a Hockey Arena for Circle Campus." I was stunned. It was hard to believe but the Trustees had, at the recommendation of President Corbally and Chancellor Riddle, approved a capital budget item to be sent to the Governor for a $10 million ice hockey arena that could also be used for basketball and rock concerts. The Polish students could play hockey and the African Americans basketball. Who needed a library? This struck me as the worst kind of racism.

Hungry and exhausted, I phoned Riddle at his condo as soon as I got home—the only time in two years I had ever phoned him at home. He was apologetic but firm. "I agreed with Corbally that this was what the campus most needed. A ranked hockey team will bring the students together and give us a national visibility. It had to take precedence over the library." I vented my distress and hung up.

Next morning at 8:45 A.M.—very early for Riddle—he came to my office, sat down and told me that I should start looking for another job.

He would give me a strong reference. I was, he said, the Ted Williams of administrators, great in my way but impossible as a team player. Maybe some other chancellor or president could tolerate me. He and Corbally certainly could not.

The previous July in a New York heat wave, and the day after a general power failure, I had been interviewed for the position of executive vice president of Yeshiva University by its President Rabbi Norman Lamm, a dignified, ascetic-looking, and very literate man, on the more modern or liberal wing of Jewish orthodoxy. I had been discovered by a headhunting firm that Lamm had retained. It was not hard to find me. How many Jews had taught at Yeshiva, where I had inspired the students, both men and women, was a well-known scholar, and was vice president of a large university? That put me in a pool of one. Lamm indicated that he was prepared to offer me the job. A year later I would have jumped at the offer, but after only one year at Circle, I was reluctant to move. And there was a stumbling block. I would not really be executive vice president of the whole university. The Albert Einstein Medical Center in the Bronx would be outside my jurisdiction. Yet Einstein was the one part of Yeshiva University that had money and a very good national reputation.

I was being brought in to do a salvage job on the other motley units of the University, those which were underfunded and understaffed and had only modest reputations. I flew back to Chicago and told the woman running the headhunting firm, which specialized in academic appointments, that I would not take the Yeshiva job. Now in January 1978, after being sandbagged by Riddle and Corbally, I deeply regretted that decision.

Three months later, however, found me in a promising situation again. I was one of the three finalists for the presidency of Queens College in CUNY. I had a private breakfast in March with the CUNY chancellor at the University Club on Fifth Avenue. He told me that I was his choice, but his appointment of me would have to be held off for a few weeks while he dealt with a political problem: another candidate, the acting president of Queens College, had the support of the Queens borough president and the chancellor would have to mollify this politician before proceeding with the appointment.

I felt good about this. I went back to Chicago and started to clean up my files. One secretary I had asked early into my job to come in at 7:00 A.M. because that is when I started dictating letters and memos. Now I said to her, "By the way, where do you live?"

"Fort Wayne, Indiana." She had to get up at 5:00 A.M. to come to work. I felt ashamed.

A couple of days later the headhunting woman, who had heard about the Queens prospect, was on the phone again. "President John Sawhill of New York University is looking for a new dean of the Faculty of Arts and Science, a very important position at NYU. Will you talk to him?"

"Sure, why not."

Sawhill put me up in his penthouse apartment on Washington Square. I had a brief interview with an unhappy faculty search committee who had tried for six months to come up with a dean candidate Sawhill would accept but had failed to do so. Sawhill pressured them into endorsing me. He offered me the job and I accepted. I turned down CUNY—an incident that got into the *New York Times*—and the day after Memorial Day 1978, I moved into the elegant nineteenth-century office with genuine antique furniture, of the dean of the Faculty of Arts and Science at 5 Washington Square North. At the end of August my wife and daughter, who was slated to attend NYU a year later when she finished prep school, moved into the dean's renovated townhouse in fashionable Washington Mews.

I took the job at NYU instead of CUNY-Queens (the two positions paid almost the same salaries and benefits) because of the politics involved in holding a presidency in an urban public university. First of all, the Queens borough president (who later committed suicide after being exposed for corruption) wanted another candidate and might wage guerrilla warfare against me. Secondly, the part of my job at Circle that I had handled poorly was dealing with the African American community and I could see myself failing in the racial category again at CUNY in New York.

Like all urban universities with substantial black and Hispanic minorities, Circle ran a remediation program (TYP, or Transitional Year Program). It was costly—a million dollars a year in 1976 dollars—and the Faculty Council headed by Maurice Eash, an expert in evaluating educational programs, thought TYP was of little or no use in preparing minority students for the regular college curriculum. The issue got in the newspapers: The *Chicago Tribune* raged that the Circle president and provost should stop wasting this public money on minorities. Riddle handed this hot potato to me to attend to and got out of the way.

I decided to go and see the director of the remediation program, who had offices on the other side of the campus, and review the situation with him. When I got to his office there was a huge burgundy Cadillac with gold trim outside his door. He was a big black man; he looked like a former football player. "That is quite a car outside," I began.

"Yes, it's mine," he said with a smile. "I lease it and charge it to the University."

Then as he started to sit down I saw he was carrying a gun in a holster. "Why are you carrying sidearms on the campus?"

"There are some tough kids in this program," he said.

A half-hour into the conversation convinced me that improvement of the program should start with the hiring of a new director—an educator, which the current director was clearly not. I went back to my office and read his personnel file to find out how he had been appointed five years previously. It was a political appointment from the Democratic (Black) machine on the South Side. I made an appointment to go down to the Democratic clubhouse and talk to the current boss of the organization, the African American alderman named Harold Washington (later mayor). I delicately explained the TYP situation and requested that Alderman Washington offer the director a job in his organization on the South Side. "Hell, no," he said, "we were trying to get rid of that jerk for years. I was delighted to palm him off on the Circle Campus with Mayor Daley's help. I don't want that lazy bugger around here again."

Pressed by Maurice Eash and the Faculty Council to do something, I boldly found an experienced black educator at Michigan State to take over direction of the remediation program. I held a press conference to announce that the remediation program would go on but under new direction and with higher standards. The gun-toting director left quietly for a job at Malcolm X University. The *Chicago Tribune* lavished praise on me—a provost with courage at last.

I felt good until 6:00 A.M. the next morning as I stood at a bus stop in fifteen above weather and put a quarter in a newspaper vending machine to see how I did in the *Chicago Sun-Times*—they ignored the matter. Next to it was a vending machine selling the African American newspaper, *The Defender.* Through the glass I could see the headlines denouncing me as a racist. A day later someone detonated a smoke bomb under my car. I never dared tell my wife that.

Riddle said I had mishandled the whole thing. Calling a press conference was a huge mistake. "Things like this happened every month at John Jay College in New York. I refused to talk to the press and it always blew over." I was hauled before the university's Board of Trustees and publicly reprimanded for exactly what I never understood—putting them in a hotspot and making them late for the opening curtain of a musical comedy, I suppose. Even the suburban matron on the Board, who a few months earlier had made a pass at me, criticized me. Maybe she resented that I had not succumbed to her North Shore charms.

NYU's minority enrollment was only 5 percent and was mostly congregated in the Education School, so I wouldn't have to face the racial problem there—and I didn't. Nor did I have problems with the faculty as at Binghamton. In the spring of 1999, while a search for a fourth dean of faculty since I was fired in April 1981 was going on, two faculty members, the Henry James Professor of Letters, the Irish critic Denis Donoghue, and the director of Ireland House, the historian Robert Scally, approached me while I was eating ribs at a bar on University Place and asked me to join them. I demurred. "You know," said Scally, "you were the best dean we ever had. We never got another one like you."

I hired Denis Donoghue while three other universities were after him after he decided to leave his chair at University College, Dublin. I also hired Annette Weiner, the anthropologist (later dean of the Graduate School) from Texas-Austin and the Princeton philosopher, Tom Nagel, one of the half dozen leading philosophers of his generation. In 1980 the NYU Philosophy Department rated something like 200th in the country. Today, under Tom Nagel's leadership, it rates first. I also recruited to mend the sick Biology Department, as its Chair, the rising star of the Rockefeller University, William Beers. He had a laser beam mind and a personality to go with it. He later became the Vice President for Research at Rockefeller University.

I remember the day Beers first visited the campus and I sent him over to the Biology Department to evaluate its research facilities. He was back in fifteen minutes. "Dreadful," he said. I asked him how he could make such a quick assessment. "Fish tanks," Beers said, "the place is full of fish tanks, but they don't have one electron microscope. They are doing nineteenth-century science." Of course he was right on the mark. How a group of scientists hate to be shown what they are doing is thoroughly obsolete and useless. Remember the Binghamton Rube-Goldberg physicists? The NYU biologists in 1979 were not much better.

For the first time under my leadership, NYU Arts and Science competed for quality faculty at the Ivy League level. This transformed not only the national image of the place but also the faculty's view of themselves. They knew that they were in the Big Show now, not at old also-ran tumbledown NYU. This kind of transformation is the most important thing an administrator can accomplish, and it is also the most difficult.

What it takes to upgrade a university is not only the application of increased funding. There has to occur an improvement in faculty morale and the development of a sense among the faculty of collectively engaging in the pursuit of excellence in teaching as well as research. I cannot say I achieved this fully as dean at NYU for three years, but I made a start. It is a transformation not necessarily welcomed by all officers in the central administration on a campus. Extensive development along the line of high morale and a sense of cohesiveness will give a dean in the long run great power to summon faculty support when he needs it, including support against the campus central administration. A president, chancellor, or vice president might not want to see a dean marshaling such power. He must be stopped before he diminishes the capacity of campus central administration to make deals with particular Departments, institutes, and faculty. Such resentment certainly developed towards me at NYU.

I did other important things in my three-year tenure as NYU dean of Arts and Science (the last two years also as dean of the Graduate School). For the first time the faculty of Arts and Science had a budget and it was a PPB operation. The dean previous to me did not believe in budgets. He never knew a week from the end of the fiscal year whether he was two million in the red or two million in the black. It was invariably the latter and the wily Vice President for Finance in Central Administration, Alan Claxton, never told him, being delighted to get the unused money back.

Major upgrading of the faculty and facilities of the Biology, Economics, and Sociology Departments were undertaken. I had a meeting with the whole English Department and told them that their present foci on literary biography and 1930s' style New Criticism (close reading of texts) wasn't enough. They needed faculty committed to the new kind of postmodernist literary theory, to deconstruction. Most of the senior faculty were furious with me but they began to recruit the new kind of faculty and set the NYU English Department on the road to what it is today, one of the best in the country and a magnet for first-rate graduate students.

A complete equity and merit review of faculty salaries was completed, resulting in large merit rewards to exceptional teachers and to the grossly underpaid women faculty. A woman psychology professor was not only given a big raise but a cash award of $6,000 if she would sign a paper promising not to sue the university; with a shocked look after years of mistreatment, she signed.

I provided funding for faculty interdisciplinary seminars and I instituted a policy that when a faculty member received a Guggenheim Fellowship or appointment as a visiting professor at Oxbridge, we made up the difference between their modest stipends or salary and their NYU salary. I tried to introduce paid paternity as well as maternity leave for faculty but was stopped and reprimanded by the university counsel. I got the Liberal Arts M.A. program for mature adults off the ground. It made a lot of money for the university. I brought in Arthur Williamson from Chicago to run the program. He was an excellent scholar with an entrepreneurial temperament. I also taught my own college course on the common law.

When Sawhill offered me the job in April 1978, I accepted on only one condition, that he promise he would stay as president of NYU for the next three years. He promised but stayed for only one, going on extended leave to become Deputy Secretary for Energy in the Carter Administration, with the proviso that he would be the Energy Secretary after Carter's reelection (which, of course, didn't happen).

I was surprised that Sawhill was serving in a Democratic administration. I thought of him, with his devotion to market economy, as a slightly right of center Republican. He was always talking about his friends on Wall Street. But Sawhill turned out to have a liberal side—conservation and environmental protection—under the influence of his formidable and brilliant wife, the head of an urban studies think tank in Washington. Belle Sawhill visited the NYU campus only once a year and made clear she didn't think much of it.

New York University was founded at almost the same time as the University of London—London in 1836, NYU officially in 1831, but classes really began there in 1843 with the building of Old Main on Washington Square. If you look at the plaque commemorating Old Main, you will see that most donors had Dutch names. Similar to the University of London, NYU was intended to provide an up-to-date secular education for the middle class at a modest tuition.

Until the early twentieth century NYU loped along earning no particular distinction except for the presence on its faculty of Samuel Morse, the developer of the electrical telegraph, who was professor of both physics and painting and was also renowned for being a racist and an anti-Semite, and William Draper, a pioneering historian of science.

With the vast tide of Jewish immigration into Lower Manhattan in the late nineteenth century, the college at Washington Square began to attract an unseemly number of Jews. The Trustees took two actions. They established a pristine, well-designed new campus on University Heights in the Bronx, overlooking the Harlem River. It was restricted to men and a rigid quota of 15 percent Jews was established for student admissions, which lasted until the post-World War II period. The Heights Campus was, with the help of state money, closed down in 1973 and became the campus of Bronx Community College. Its arts and science faculty was at that time transferred down to Washington Square and its large engineering faculty sold to Brooklyn Polytech.

Meanwhile colorful events had been happening on the coed old Washington Square campus. The Trustees decided to milk it as a fee paying, mediocre-quality college for immigrant Jews and in the 1920s it was referred to as "NY Jew." The elegant nineteenth-century Gothic instructional building on Washington Square East, Old Main, was torn down and in its place was erected an ugly ten-story warehouse-type structure. The top three floors of the building were used by the University and the bottom seven floors were leased to a book publisher (the whole ugly thing, many times renovated, now houses the College of Arts and Science).

A building nearby, a sweatshop where the notorious Triangle Shirtwaist Factory fire of 1903 occurred (killing three hundred young Jewish women) was bought by the university, slightly renovated, and also used as an instructional building. More buildings adjoining and near the Square were added between the wars and in the 1940s and 1950s as NYU became the place where middle-class immigrants of any ethnicity sent their sons and daughters if they wanted to avoid the free but grim city colleges.

NYU even had a football team of some quality for a while and a championship postwar basketball team until some of its players, all Jewish, confessed to taking bribes from gamblers. NYU had no library building until 1971. Then Bobst Library, one of Philip Johnson's less successful brutalities, was opened, funded by a New Jersey pharmaceutical manufacturer of somewhat dubious reputation.

The NYU faculty was catch as catch can, depending on the enterprise of chairmen and the whims of deans. It had interesting intellectuals teaching there: the then-Marxist philosopher Sidney Hook and even the novelist Tom Wolfe (*Look Homeward, Angel*) for a while. In 1938 its

History Department was full of brilliant young scholars, most of whom were lured away in the following decade: its stars Henry Steele Commager to Columbia and Wallace K. Ferguson back to Canada.

NYU in the 1960s and 1970s was known as a place whose only entry requirement was literacy. If you (or your parents) could write a tuition check, you were admitted. Yet it was an easy-going, comfortable environment in dynamic Greenwich Village where a good education could be obtained without fuss and bother. The French, comparative literature, mathematics, and art History Departments were highly ranked nationally.

One of the best things that ever happened to NYU was serendipitous. After the War, Metropolitan Life had built a huge apartment complex two blocks south of the campus. They found it unprofitable and sold it off to NYU for a song. This provided cheap faculty housing and drew to the faculty scholars and writers who otherwise might not have been there.

NYU's president in the early 1970s when the Heights Campus was sold off as the south Bronx deteriorated was a handsome, well-spoken, easygoing man, a prexy from Central Casting, who did not believe in budgets. Before the annual Trustees meeting on the budget, he dictated to the Vice President for Finance his conception of what an attractive budget ought to look like and gave this fiction to the Trustees.

The venerable chairman of the Board of Trustees, the investment banker John Loeb, finally got rid of this charming gentleman and in 1974 hired John Sawhill, whom he knew on Wall Street, as president—against the wishes of the faculty.

❖ ❖ ❖

John Sawhill was not your garden-variety president. He was a tall, gaunt man, a diabetic, and a fitness and diet fanatic. When I worked for Sawhill he was still in his forties. He was different from any other university president I have ever known or heard about, but in his idiosyncratic and unconventional manner he was a very good president for NYU, and he turned the place around and launched it from mediocrity to high respectability. He was not an easy man to like, but I liked and admired him even though he could be exasperatingly off the wall. When I had my job interview with Sawhill he claimed he took a course with me at Princeton in 1958 and received an "A." I had no recollection of him whatsoever.

Sawhill had obtained a Ph.D. from the NYU Business School and went to work on Wall Street. That was his world and the corporate giants in investment banking and venture capital (like Loeb) were his gods, whose mannerisms he tried to emulate.

For instance, he had gotten the idea somehow that among corporation officers only the Chief Executive Officer wore a very dark navy suit, as only the emperor in old Constantinople wore the imperial purple. Presumably his vice presidents and deans were supposed to wear gray stripe. Noticing this clothing color policy, I baited him by turning up at a deans' meeting with the president in a dark navy worsted suit almost identical to his. He was visibly upset and glowered at me through the meeting. The next meeting I wore a checkered brown sports jacket and he was much happier.

He knew how universities worked but sometimes he simply forgot, or pretended to forget, and acted as one of those outrageously tyrannical corporate CEO's he so much admired. One Saturday he phoned me at home and announced that the previous evening at a dinner party he had discovered that a tenured full professor in the NYU Politics Department, Berthold Ollman, was a Communist. Certainly a left wing Marxist, I replied. "Get rid of him," Sawhill shouted. I told him I would look into this grave matter immediately.

I phoned the university counsel and said, "Andy, would you please phone John Sawhill immediately and remind him about the First and Fourteenth Amendments and that NYU officially adheres to the AAUP rules on academic freedom and tenure, and that there is no way in God's creation we can get rid of Bert Ollman?"

S. Andrew Schaffer sighed. "Not that again. I'll phone John."

Another behavioral mannerism Sawhill picked up from the corporate world was the CEO's address to the whole staff. Because the university lacked the media transmittal for this totalitarian performance, he insisted in going to the first faculty meeting of the year in each school and addressing the faculty workers. I told him that as far as Arts and Science was concerned, it was a waste of time because very few of the 350 faculty attended the monthly faculty meetings—unlike Princeton and Columbia. He persisted, so I sent a memo to the whole faculty telling them of Sawhill's upcoming performance and would they please turn up. I was surprised when fifty faculty actually showed.

Sawhill was disappointed in the tepid applause that he got. He blamed it on his speech, something about the essence of liberal education. He assigned me to write a better speech and delivered it at the first faculty meeting of the next semester to a slightly better response. Encouraged by this, he published the speech in *The Atlantic Monthly* under his name. I didn't mind the plagiarism but I had more important things to do than serve as the president's speechwriter. I recommended that instead of relying on hacks in the Public Relations Office and deans to write his speeches, he hire Zane Berzins, a former student of mine at Barnard who was an excellent journalist and literary critic. He did so and was very satisfied with the results. For eight months Zane drove around with him in his town car (he never used a limousine because it was too ostentatious and burned too much fossil fuel) ready to produce prose at any time. I never told him that Zane was as far left as Bert Ollman.

Sawhill died of diabetes in 2001 at the age of sixty-three. In the previous fifteen years he had been the national head of the Nature Conservancy. Far more than any president I ever worked with, Sawhill could take severe criticism and not resent it. He had a job to do and that was the important point. He wanted to take a disorganized, slack, second-rate university and make it first-rate and well administered. He left too soon (he served only from 1974 to 1980) but remarkably he turned the sloppy, old NYU ship around, put it in much better shape, and set NYU on the road to being a very good university with many distinguished units and a draw to students from all over the country. Of the university presidents I have known, he was the only one I would go to work for again at the drop of a hat—and that is the ultimate criterion of leadership.

Sawhill's confidante and chief adviser was the Vice President for Student Services, Jane Maggin. She came from a wealthy New York Irish family, got an M.A. in history from NYU, entered the university administration at a humble level and slowly worked her way up by dint of her tremendous energy, common sense, and devotion to students. Her portfolio was much broader than her title. She was in effect Sawhill's gray eminence. She believed that the key to NYU's future lay in the building of many high-class dormitories for students. I supported her in this view.

In the 1990s the current president, Jay Oliva, and the Board of Trustees had the courage to take thirty million dollars normally slated for the university's endowment and make this capital investment in student housing. It has made a big difference in NYU's image and the composition of its student body. The dormitories, like the fourteen-story one on Union Square with a splendid dining hall, should be named after Sawhill and Maggin. They started it all.

At the end of my fourth month as dean, at a faculty retreat in Westchester, Sawhill took me for a moonlight walk in the woods and told me he saw me as his eventual successor. Then within a couple of months he heard from his provost, Jay Oliva, and Jane Maggin, that I was not a team player and he never mentioned this anointment to me again. Indeed half a year after I began, his executive committee of vice presidents told him I was a troublemaker and should be fired. But Sawhill did not listen to them. He knew he needed me.

Under pressure from the new chairman of the Board of Trustees, real estate and entertainment billionaire Laurence Tisch, a NYU alumnus, Sawhill in the summer of 1980 designated the dean of the Medical School (which Tisch lavishly admired and funded), Ivan Bennett, as acting president while Sawhill was in Washington. I had seen Bennett operate at Council of Deans' meetings with Sawhill and I thought Ivan Bennett a thug, a liar, and probably a crook. He came to NYU in 1972 from Washington D.C. where he was a senior officer in the National Institutes of Health. He was widely reputed to be America's leading expert on germ warfare.

From the first deans' meeting I attended in September 1978, it was clear that the Medical School and its surrounding Medical Center (two hospitals) were in deep fiscal trouble and were running big deficits. Bennett blamed this on Governor Carey, who had cut back on state support for the hospitals and then on the federal government which followed suit. I had no doubt this had happened but the deficits were too large for this to be the only cause.

In any case it was the responsibility of the head of a university medical center to adjust to shifting patterns in funding from state and federal sources. Through the 1960s and 1970s medical schools and their teaching hospitals were favorite targets of public largess. They became used to constant expansion. They showed budget surpluses which at NYU the Medical Center never shared with the impoverished Arts and Science school. Now there was a downturn in the public funding of medical education and research, which has continued to the present day. Bennett, a pugnacious and arrogant man, did not want to accept this altered situation. He was furious that Sawhill had committed the University to improvement in the school of Arts and Science at a time when the Medical Center was running budgetary deficits. He looked upon me as at best a naïve humanist who did not understand where funding priorities should lie on the campus.

Bennett reeked of the con man. I made discreet inquiries from the chair of the NYU Biology Department to the departmental chair of psychiatry at the Medical School. Bennett had hired some thirty high-salaried tenured faculty on soft money—that is, on government grants. As the grants ran out, these faculty came onto the Medical School's budget along with their expensive labs and flooded it with red ink. If some administrator had done this in a state university, he would have been indicted for fraud.

Of course Sawhill and his provost, L. Jay Oliva, knew about all this but were afraid of Bennett as protected by Tisch. They did nothing. Bennett kept talking grandly at deans' meetings about a forthcoming monstrously big legacy soon to come to the Medical School from a sick old lady in New Jersey. My inquiries revealed that she was old, but scarcely on her deathbed and in any case the legacy was at most six million while the Medical School's debt was many times that.

Bennett had to be appointed acting president as a cover-up. If another dean had been appointed, like me or the dean of the Law School, he would have immediately discovered Bennett's malfeasance and the cover-up. Tisch would not have wanted such information discreditable to the Medical School and its dean made public. As McGeorge Bundy once explained to me, "At Harvard the Trustees are devoted to the undergraduate college because their students days there were among the happiest of their lives. Even if the NYU Trustees are alumni, they have no special memories of the place. They are old Jews trying to stay alive and counting on the Medical Center to help them out." NYU's teaching hospital is now indeed named after Laurence Tisch.

For two years as Sawhill got an extension of leave, Bennett and I circled each other like two wild animals looking for an opening for the kill, while Oliva acted as low-key intermediary. Then two things happened early in 1981 in quick succession.

First, I discovered that Bennett had instructed the Vice President for Finance, Alan Claxton, to take the surplus I had carefully built up in the Arts and Science budget for program development and more graduate student aid and to transfer the money toward the deficit in the Medical School. I confronted Bennett at a deans' meeting and there was a terrible row. I lost my temper. "If you go on this way," I shouted down the conference table, "I will take up the matter with the state attorney general." I was angry but not crazy. New York State is—thanks to a law written by Alexander Hamilton—the only state in the union in which the attorney general can investigate maladministration in a private university (he did this most recently in 1997, removing the president—my old Brandeis dean, Peter Diamandopoulos—and all but one member of the Board of Trustees of Adelphi University for misconduct).

The second event was that Tisch and the Board refused to extend Sawhill's leave for a third year and he submitted his resignation. There was now a campus search committee to advise Tisch and the Trustees on the selection of a new president. I was one of the two deans elected to the search committee. Bennett threw his hat in the ring immediately and seemed to be a shoo-in. I looked around for a strong candidate to put up against him. I chose Vartan Gregorian, a former dean of Arts and Science at the University of Pennsylvania, later to be the phenomenally successful head of the New York Public Library and a less illustrious president of Brown University. He was a man of vision and unlimited energy as well as a very good historian.

Tisch vetoed Vartan Gregorian. His name was held to be "too Arabic" (he was, in fact, a Christian Armenian American) and that would frighten off Jewish donors. I returned to my office facing the gloomy prospect of Bennett becoming president. I ghost-wrote a long article in *The Village Voice* disparaging Bennett but that wouldn't stop him.

Then I got a call from an old Columbia College student, Sanford Greenberg, now a prominent venture capitalist in Washington. He said he was speaking for his friend and close associate in the Democratic Party, John Brademas, who had after twenty years recently lost his seat in Congress. "John intends to apply for the NYU job, and he needs your help, and you know politicians are always loyal to those who help them." Two days later I was having a three-hour lunch with Brademas in a Greek restaurant two blocks from the Capitol.

He seemed to be an intelligent, decent, and articulate person. He was a Rhodes scholar and had a D.Phil. in modern history from Oxford.

He had taught for three years at a small college in Indiana before entering Congress. Yet I was amazed by his total ignorance of how a large university worked or even how a college president was selected. Of NYU he knew almost nothing. I had no alternative but to make him my candidate, even though in my view he ranked far below Gregorian. At least he was not Bennett, and Greenberg had assured me that politicians have long and undying loyalty memories.

In the next month I had three long face-to-face meetings with Brademas at the apartment of a friend of his in Manhattan, as well as a half dozen follow-up phone calls he made to me at my home in the evening. Like all successful politicians he was a quick if superficial study. With my coaching, Brademas did well on his hour-long interview with the search committee. He looked good, spoke with confidence, and knew what he was talking about—an ideal president.

The night before the Search Committee was to meet and make its recommendation to Tisch, a strange thing happened. John Sawhill phoned me at 10:30 P.M. from Washington. He was very wound up; I thought he had been drinking. "Norman, I know the Search Committee is meeting tomorrow morning on its final decision to give to Tisch. I want you to tell the Search Committee to nominate me to Tisch. I am much better than John Brademas."

I was stunned. When I found my speech, I stuttered "I have no doubt you are better than Brademas, John. But at this point in the proceedings, I can't suddenly raise your name. The only one who can bring your name forward at this point is Tisch himself. Why don't you call Tisch and talk to him? If he comes to the Committee and asks our opinion about you, I will switch from Brademas to you. I don't know what the others on the Committee will do."

There was a long pause. I thought I heard Sawhill crying. "I deserve to come back as president."

"Probably you do, John, but I cannot put this forward now; only Tisch can." There was another long pause and Sawhill put the phone down.

The Committee did not hear from Tisch about Sawhill the next day. We were down to two candidates, Brademas and Bennett. As a result of Brademas' impressive performance at his interview, his distinguished public record, and the lobbying of myself and the other dean on the Committee, the Search Committee reported to Tisch that Brademas was our first choice and we were divided on Bennett. Tisch said he would think about it and consult with the godfather, old man Loeb. Three days later Brademas' selection was approved and Bennett summoned me to his president's office.

I went with dread. With glee Bennett told me that he had the approval of Tisch and Brademas to demand my resignation within twenty-four hours or I would be summarily fired. I asked him for the reasons for my dismissal and he gave none. I asked him whether my family could continue to occupy the dean's house in Washington Mews. Bennett glowered and replied: "Of course not. We'll find a small apartment for you elsewhere." Dazed but not altogether surprised, I went home and told my wife and daughter and phoned my mother in Winnipeg; she was unsympathetic.

I summoned an emergency meeting of the Arts and Science faculty executive committee. I told them there were two ways to go. First, they could stand by me and we would publicly fight this. Or secondly, they could do nothing and I would try to cut the best deal I could with the University. They sent me home around the corner and went into secret session. Ninety minutes later two members of the committee, the chairs of journalism and sociology, rang my doorbell and said: "Cut your deal, Norman. We won't fight this." I strongly suspected that at least the journalism chair had cut his own deal with NYU for deserting me.

First I scheduled a meeting with Brademas for the next day; he had just come up from D.C. to hold a triumphant press conference. I did not ask him how and why he had betrayed me but he volunteered. "Bennett would only accept my appointment if Tisch and I gave him authority to fire you. He sure hates you. Tisch said I had to agree to your dismissal or no presidency for me. I need this job badly."

I rose to leave and said: "My lawyers will be talking to you. Good luck."

I phoned William D. Zabel, senior partner in a leading New York law firm. I said, "Bill, remember back in 1958 at Princeton when my wife and I were kind and comforting to you when you were taking hell from the anti-Semites and you said, Professor Cantor, if you are ever in real trouble, call on me immediately? Well, Bill, that day has arrived." I told him what had happened.

Zabel said, "Don't leave your office. I will be there in half an hour." He immediately made an appointment with the University Counsel, Andy Schaffer, for later that afternoon and turned up at my office with two associates.

The three grilled me as to where I might be vulnerable. I said that my campus record was sparkling clean and I was popular with the great majority of the faculty. On the downside two years before I had a three-month affair with a young woman who worked in the University. "Did Sawhill know about this?" Zabel said.

"I presume so," I said, "because the President's Office paid for the woman's therapy and then Sawhill got the therapist, Dr. Steve Ruma, to tell him everything about our relationship she had revealed to him in analysis. Ruma himself told me this. Ruma works at the Medical Center and is a pal of Bennett's." The lawyers looked at me with pity and clucked in dismay. There was a long silence.

Finally Zabel said, "We can't get your job back, but we can work out a good settlement. Don't worry."

They left for Andy Schaffer's office across the park. About ninety minutes later they were back, Zabel was smiling. "We cut a good deal," he said. "You can keep the dean's house in the Mews. You can keep the dean's salary but you will have no raise for two years. You will be in the History Department (in which I had tenure) but you won't have to teach any course you don't want to. And you can also teach elsewhere in the university. You will have a special research and book budget for five years. You will have fifteen months leave with full pay starting immediately. On the downside, NYU won't pay my legal fee because Schaffer thinks that would acknowledge that NYU was in the wrong in firing you." I expressed my undying gratitude to Bill Zabel. He said, "It was easy. Brademas told Oliva and Schaffer to give you everything you wanted."

"Nice guy, Brademas," I said. "A real sweetheart."

In December 1998 William Zabel had his sixtieth birthday dinner in a posh restaurant in Soho. He asked me to be the main speaker and talk seriously about liberal education for a half-hour. Laurence and Billie Tisch sat at the table immediately in front of the podium. Zabel was their estate and probate lawyer. Afterwards they shook my hand and told me what a fine address it was. I looked into Laurence Tisch's eyes to see if there was some memory of what had happened in the spring of 1981. There was none. Like a Mafia don, he had forgotten about the small fry he had eliminated.

A year after I was dismissed Ivan Bennett was forced out of the deanship of the NYU Medical School. He returned to research. In the late 1980s he died under mysterious circumstances in a Tokyo hotel.

At noon on May 28, 1981, Zabel's junior associate handed me the legal agreement with NYU, countersigned by Oliva, which would govern the rest of my years at the university. My wife and I got into our Volkswagen Rabbit and headed for a week's vacation at an oceanfront motel with studio apartments in Amagansett, Long Island. I cooked all the dinners for the week. Each evening I sat on the deck and as dusk rolled in ruminated on my tempestuous seven years as a university administrator.

I knew that I had acted rashly many times and demonstrated an impolitic temperament. But on the whole I felt a sense of satisfaction. I had positively affected the development of three institutions. I had obtained a hockey arena for Chicago Circle.

In the case of NYU my impact was so positive that in 1985 the Public Relations Office published an article in a university alumni magazine outlining my accomplishments but attributing them to the incumbent dean of Arts and Science. Enraged, I confronted the head of the Public Relations Office.

"Why did you do this?" I demanded.

"Because Chancellor Oliva told us to," he said. I was an unperson in Oliva's eyes, like Trotsky in Stalinist Russia.

There were a couple of matters left over from my provost and dean days that required further attention. One was trying to help the career of my chief associate at Binghamton and NYU, Judith Pitney. She came from a prominent family in Saratoga, New York. I had hired her out of Caspar Weinberger's Department of Health, Education, and Welfare first to develop federal grant proposals but eventually at NYU to be associate dean and run the dean's office. She was the most skillful program budget analyst I have ever encountered. But she was also extraordinarily skillful at dealing with two very different constituencies a dean's office has to live with: the architects and construction companies who improved our capital facilities and the mastodons and jackals who normally comprised the department chairpersons. She actually got nearly all of the chairs over time to read their budgets and operate within them. Many found that they had more resources in their budgets than they realized. Judith also taught them how you could put twelve faculty on nine faculty lines by juggling grants and leaves. Some of the science chairs knew about this legerdemain; to most of the humanities chairs it came as a revelation.

In the summer and fall of 1981, I had to help Judith Pitney find a new job. She became associate provost at Southern Methodist University in Dallas. From there she went to the University of Michigan's doctoral program in higher education management, the best such program in the country. After getting her Ph.D., she stayed in Ann Arbor to become Director of Budget and Planning in the School of Engineering, where she managed a two hundred million dollar annual budget and supervised the design and building of the finest academic building I have ever seen. I sometimes hear people say that Sawhill and Cantor turned junky old NYU around. But a lot of credit for this critical transformation should go to Jane Maggin and Judith Pitney, who became very close personal friends.

That today NYU can compete successfully with Columbia for recruitment of top flight senior faculty and its undergraduate college has become selective in its admission standards and is drawing students from all over the country was the work of many people. I was just one of them.

I also collaborated in the curricular radicalization and leftist educational trend on American campuses, at both Binghamton and New York University. I was concerned about the outcome of this political shift in educational content on the campus. But I associated the left with the new culture that I had favored and helped to foster. I had in the 1970s decreasing residual respect for the old academic culture and its connection to cultural and political conservatism. I felt that the old academic culture had failed to deliver on its promise because its proponents were doing nothing to combat the high level of unemployment among new Ph.D.s.

My support for the campus left was also conditioned by my friendship with the brilliant Terence Hopkins. Robert Merton's disciples in historical sociology at Columbia, Immanuel Wallerstein and Terence Hopkins, were the faculty leaders who supported the radical activist students on Morningside Heights in May 1968. For this each became *persona non grata* to their departmental colleagues. They went into exile—Wallerstein to teach in Montreal, Hopkins to do research in the West Indies. Dean Peter Vukasin, ever on the lookout for first-class talent, brought Hopkins to Binghamton in 1973 to upgrade the woebegone Sociology Department.

Hopkins and I became good friends. We watched endless football and baseball games on television together. In 1973 when Wallerstein first presented his thesis on economic world systems to the national meeting of sociologists in New Orleans, Hopkins arranged to have me as one of the three commentators. I gave it a mixed assessment. Wallerstein claimed that beginning in the early sixteenth century the whole world economy was joined together so as to make the non-European countries economic dependents and exploitees of Western Europe. It was the old Hobson-Lenin theory of imperialism renovated and applied to earlier times.

When Wallerstein's first of three volumes expounding this neo-Marxist world history appeared in 1974, it was immediately awarded the highest medal of the American Sociological Association.

Wallerstein made several visits to Binghamton from Montreal at Hopkins' invitation. His personality was very different from that of the diffident, shy, witty Hopkins. Wallerstein wanted to be a powerbroker, a grand patron in the French manner (he eventually got a joint appointment in Paris as well as Binghamton) and he was not reticent or delicate about his intense ambitions. I thought Wallerstein a second-class thinker and personally untrustworthy.

Yet in 1975 when Hopkins informed me that Wallerstein would come to Binghamton and chair the Sociology department if I as provost would get a permanent state funding line for a research and training institute in historical sociology, I immediately flew to Albany and got a special budget line inserted that funded the Fernand Braudel Center, named after the eminent but intellectually ambivalent and protean French historical sociologist who came for the opening ceremonies.

That was in 1977 when I had already left for Chicago. I did not come back for the opening because while Hopkins and Wallerstein had promised me that their Braudel Center would not be exclusively Marxist, it was that and then some. Because of me the long-suffering taxpayers of New York ended up paying year after year for perhaps the most left-wing institute in the country. Mistake number one.

Mistake number two was giving NYU's "dead-white-male" History Department three new faculty lines if they would appoint women. They did with alacrity, but in interviewing the department's nominees it was obvious that two of the three were very far to the left. I shut my eyes and signed off on these appointments. The two have over time both served as chairs of the now vibrant NYU History Department, but I shudder to think of what they teach their students.

I was caught in a conundrum. I was a pioneer of the new academic culture and I fought for it against the old humanism in which I was educated. Then in the seventies and eighties I watched the new academic culture being taken over by the left and its ideologies and its language transformed into a vehicle for Marxist indoctrination.

In the 1980s I tried to countervail by joining up with the neo-conservatives of the Hilton Kramer variety and contributed to his journal, *The New Criterion*. I did not enjoy membership in the ranks of the neo-cons. I found them deficient in learning, subtlety, and humor. Yet I have not gone back to swooning over classical and medieval texts. I still in my writing and teaching owe much to Marx, Freud, and Nietzsche and their French disciples of the sixties, seventies, and eighties, Claude Lévi-Strauss, Michel Foucault, and Jacques Derrida. All the books I published in the 1990s bear their influence.

My third mistake was of a more structural kind. I did not understand that the age of strong leadership in university administration was passing. With the increasing political polarization of the campus into effete moderates and strong leftists, the McGeorge Bundy type of dean, with his strong opinions and his hands-on involvement, was becoming unfashionable. The administrators who had long and successful careers were now those like John Corbally at Urbana or Jay Oliva at NYU. They were low-key bureaucrats who massaged the system but did not get involved in it and they never expressed a political opinion. I was much too involved, too hot a personality, too cerebral.

Corbally and Oliva were post-1960s administrators. Day-to-day tinkering, oiling the machinery and tightening a few bolts here and there, dressing well and making nice little meaningless speeches, and a devotion to team sports—football for Corbally at Urbana, basketball for Oliva at NYU—these were the actions that offended no one and fostered a reputation for wisdom and reliability.

What I did not understand was that leadership on campuses had passed from the activist deans to those whom I now call the icons and powerbrokers among the faculty. In a confused way, David Riesman and Christopher Jencks had foreseen this in their 1968 book *The Academic Revolution*. I thought the book was boring and irrelevant, but I was wrong. Riesman and Jencks were right on target in predicting the passing of power and decision-making on the elite fifty or so campuses to a select circle of faculty. What they did not foresee was the preponderance of the left among the elite faculty.

It was possible to be an icon and not want to be a powerbroker. And sometimes a powerbroker lacked the intellectual status of an academic icon. But usually the two roles ran together. They existed simultaneously in the same academic person.

An icon was a scholar or scientist whose work and theories had gained them magical reputations. They had become reified into cultural idols. Their work was thoroughly mastered by graduate students and some undergraduates and debated at special sessions at academic conferences. They were constantly in demand for public lectures off their own campus. "Ism" became attached to their surnames, and their names were wielded as mortal swords in academic debate.

Powerbrokers commanded patronage. In his wonderful book on French academic life Terry Clark called them grand patrons. They not only controlled a larger than normal raft of graduate fellowships and teaching and research assistantships, but they were also very successful in placing their Ph.D's in the best jobs. They had at their disposal the dream rewards for academia—the visiting professorships or research appointments for a semester or for a year or two that gave the academic beneficiaries freedom to get away from the hubbub of their own campuses, and often their aging spouses, and go elsewhere, be graciously treated and well fed, and be given the secretarial support to write the books that would make them more visible on their own campuses or, *mirabile dictu*, transform them into icons themselves and possibly powerbrokers in their own right.

Far from the leftist professors in the 1970s and 1980s protesting against the inequitable patronage system and professional cronyism, they relished it and made very skillful use of it in advancing their careers and gathering around themselves a coterie of grateful myrmidons.

The greatest success story of the icon/powerbroker was that of Lawrence Stone of Princeton. A moderately well-known Oxford don whose career had been damaged when an Oxford colleague, the formidable Tory Hugh Trevor-Roper, seemed to establish that Stone had falsified data to sustain his Marxist paradigm of early modern English social history. Stone recuperated in the mid-sixties at that resting home of British dons, the Institute for Advanced Study. From there he moved to the other end of Tigertown as the holder of an endowed chair in the Princeton History Department whose chairman he was from 1967 to 1970.

This gave Stone some patronage to dispense but it was modest compared to what he commanded as the director of the newly founded Shelby Cullom Davis Center for social history. This institute had been lavishly endowed by a far right Princeton alumnus, Cullom Davis, a billionaire oilman. When Stone revealed that he was turning the Davis

Center into a home for sundry leftist academics from the United States and Britain, Cullom Davis, no fool, tried to get his endowment back, but the president of the university, a classicist apparatchik named Robert Goheen, would not allow it, being contrary, it was claimed, to academic freedom.

To spend a year at the Cullom Davis Institute when it was under Stone's aegis in the seventies and early eighties was a big career booster. It provided not only free time to write a book but inauguration into a coterie of leftists at Ivy League level universities who could be depended upon for glowing letters at tenure and promotion time, extravagantly positive reviews of one's monographs in disciplinary journals, and favorable peer/fear reviews of NEH and Guggenheim grant applications.

Stone handed over the directorship of the Cullom Davis Institute to Natalie Zemon Davis, also a historian of early modern European society and famed as the author of *The Return of Martin Guerre*, a somewhat fictionalized account of a celebrated sixteenth-century lawsuit on which the very good French film was based.

For twenty years Zemon Davis had a commuter marriage first from Toronto to Berkeley and then the much shorter trip from Toronto to Princeton. Zemon Davis comes from a very wealthy Detroit Jewish family. As an undergraduate at Smith, she eloped with a Communist mathematician at Harvard. In the McCarthy era they sought refuge at the University of Toronto where leftist Americans had a certain cachet. In 1991 a history journal printed a remarkable interview with Zemon Davis (who rose to become president of the American Historical Association). Natalie was asked whether it was difficult to sustain an academic commuter marriage for so long. Not at all, she said; the key is to have fully duplicated residences in both cities. Easy enough to do for the daughter of a Detroit millionaire. If Natalie actually carried out this prescription of duplicated domiciles, it must have cost a pretty penny because her house in Princeton was furnished with genuine French antiques.

After Natalie retired from Princeton and went back to teach at Toronto and be near her children and grandchildren, the directorship of the Cullom Davis Institute passed to a medievalist, one of Joe Strayer's two African American Ph.D.s, William Chester Jordan. He is an assiduous powerbroker but only moderately an icon.

The Princeton History Department story of icon and powerbroker could be repeated for a large number of academic leftists: Eric Foner at Columbia in American history (his uncle, Philip Foner, used to give "Red" speeches on Union Square in the 1930s and 1940s); Morton Horwitz, Harvard, who wrote the classic Marxist interpretation of nineteenth-century American law—the book won all sorts of prizes; Clifford Geertz in anthropology at the Institute for Advanced Study—behind the façade of "symbolic anthropology" lay a rare narrative skill; the twin masters of cultural theory (Marxist "New Historicism")—Sacvan Bercovitch (Harvard) and Stephen Greenblatt (also at Harvard); Edward Said at Columbia, literary theorist and PLO polemicist; the feminist historians Joan Scott, Linda Gordon, and Lynn Hunt respectively at the Institute for Advanced Study, NYU, and UCLA; Judith Butler, the feminist Berkeley theorist and literary critic, with a huge popular following among graduate students and winner of a prize for bad writing; Stephen Jay Gould, the Harvard biologist who did not believe in biology—all differences in intelligence are socially created; Immanuel Wallerstein, the sociologist at Binghamton who devoted his career to trashing Western Imperialism while building up his own academic empire that stretched from the Susquehanna River to the

Seine; John Rawls, political theory, Harvard, who used the old social contract theory to sustain the welfare state; and Richard Rorty, philosophy, Virginia, who revived early twentieth-century New Deal pragmatism.

Such were the most prominent of the leftist academics who by the force of their intellects, skillful promotion, and access to fleshpots of patronage built up impregnable power centers in American higher education. They had a far greater academic impact than university presidents. What they said and wrote filtered down into college classrooms everywhere. Parents paying $30,000 a year to send Michael or Marcia to Swarthmore or Harvard found their progeny coming home spouting leftist theory and wondered why.

Some of the icons and academic powerbrokers became deans, such as Catherine Stimpson and Thomas Bender at NYU or Stanley Fish at Illinois-Chicago and Annette Kolodny at the University of Arizona. But their deanships were secondary in importance to their stature as icons and their ongoing control of patronage.

Compared to these giants, I had to admit I was an ephemeral and marginal, perhaps ridiculous person. In 1988 Harvard's Sacvan Bercovitch came to give a public lecture at Tel Aviv University while I was teaching there. The lecture room was so crowded that I had to sit under a table. Sacvan (named by his Montreal Communist parents after Sacco and Vanzetti) delivered a straight-line Marxist version of American history. In the discussion afterwards I demurred from my perch under the table. Sacvan dismissed my comments with the wave of his hand and the sycophantic Israeli audience howled me into silence.

I can understand why the leftist icons and powerbrokers focus on the iron triangle of race, class, and gender they are always talking about. What I cannot understand is why they are so angry at and critical of the

United States, which treats them so well. They expect of America a moral perfectionism that no other country had come as close as the United States to achieving. I wonder if they are all trying to make up for unhappy childhoods or sexual dissatisfaction or some other psychological depravity.

There is nothing in their social situation to make them justifiably so radical and rebellious and so critical of the main contours of American history. They have flourished under the American system. They are top dogs within it. Exactly whom are they contending against? They have met the enemy and it is them.

They professed to be contending against the ghosts of Nixon and Reagan which have, however, become ephemeral and insignificant in American life. The Vietnam War never ended in their secluded psyches; they seem to be jealous of Jane Fonda's treasonous opportunity to condemn the American army from a Communist capital. Explanation for their attitudes and behavior seems to lie in the realm of psychopathology.

Two or three times a year I ventured to attend a meeting of the much improved NYU History Department faculty. I studied the faces of especially the younger faculty, who are nowadays mostly women. Their determined assent to any conceivable leftist dogma mystifies me. Perhaps it is an anthropological thing. They grew up in a leftist college culture, studied with leftist teachers in graduate school, have benefited from the patronage provided by leftist icons and powerbrokers. Within a span of eight years the presidency of the American Historical Association has been held by Natalie Zemon Davis and Eric Foner, respectively a spouse and nephew of card-carrying Communists. The young faculty radicals were immersed in a cargo cult.

All this would only be of marginal interest if these were not the teachers and role models for another generation. Sometimes I think that today's undergraduate students are really too wise and sophisticated to take seriously leftist ideology that normally spews from the lecture platform. They regurgitate it on exams to get a high grade and then forget about it. But I am not sure that this benign scenario is correct. Sometimes I walked back across the park from the History meeting very depressed.

The code of academic freedom demands, nearly all university administrators these days will say, that appointment be made on the basis of scholarly excellence irrespective of political ideology. This sounds professional and democratic and it conveniently gets the deans and presidents off the hook of having to make hard and possibly unpopular decisions.

But look a little closer and it will be seen that in faculty appointments the cards are stacked to make sure that the professor appointed is bound to be left of center. NYU until a few years ago had an excellent historian in the field of American corporate history. He wrote a very good book on the Morgan bank. He was not uncritical of it but he did present a sympathetic picture of its skillful operations. When he retired the academic line was switched to a third departmental appointment in the African American field, to an expert on "women of color." Assuredly an important field, but meanwhile there is no longer anyone in the NYU History Department equipped to teach the history of business corporations, on whose largesse the dominantly leftist faculty themselves prosper.

But business corporations, so goes the leftist mind, are inherently bad and therefore unworthy of serious study. Are the NYU President and the Dean uncaring about this significant change in the Department's curricular capability? Not uncaring so much as persistently oblivious to instructional value with political implications.

Take another case from New York University. For twenty years the head of its graduate program in American Civilization was a highly productive scholar in the field of the history of architecture. He was abruptly shunted aside a half dozen years ago and pushed toward retirement by the hiring as the head of American Civilization of a young hotshot from Princeton whose fields are rock music and gays, a timely shift, it could be said, from the old to the new academic culture.

But in the course of this academic swing, a solid middle-of-the-road liberal has been supplanted by a determined leftist who will thereby affect the kind of graduate students recruited into the program and the ideological implications of their training.

The defense of the hiring and promotion of faculty leftists at the expense of moderates and conservatives is enshrined in the canons of academic freedom. But nineteen times out of twenty (at least) in the humanities departments at leading universities today academic freedom means the appointment of a leftist. Presidents and deans know how hard it is to make an argument against this pattern, so they say nothing. This is leadership by surrender. One thinks of the old saying about the evil done in the world when the men of goodwill keep quiet.

As I sat on the deck in Amagansett in the early summer of 1981, my priority for the next decade was teaching in such a way as to countervail the leftist flood tide on the campus. I always felt as provost and dean that I could out-teach anyone on the faculty. The NYU History Department, however, was loath to have me thrown back in their midst. They had a committed feminist medievalist, Penelope D. Johnson, to train medieval graduate students and allowed me only a small role in this important work.

So I offered my services to other schools in the university. For the School of (Performing) Arts I developed a two-semester introductory course in the humanities that focused as much on film, art, and music as on literary and philosophical texts. But after three years of huge success in the program, the Performing Arts faculty told the dean to terminate my program; I was cutting too much into their areas of specialty.

For six years I taught the history of the common law in NYU's School of Law. It was well received by the Law School's brilliant students—as a group the most intellectually powerful I have ever encountered—but there too the faculty dropped me after a while. I was putting the history of law in its social and cultural contexts. They wanted a more traditional, technical, and narrow approach, and at great expense they hired the master in the field at Cambridge University to come over each fall and teach the legal history course.

In 1991 I was chosen one of the twelve best teachers in the College of Arts and Science. My reward was a piece of paper and a raise of $1,000. Right there is a key indicator of what is wrong with American higher education, why students are bored and indifferent, and why the academic profession now attracts few first-rate minds. It has no rational reward system. In a firm of three hundred and fifty Wall Street brokers or lawyers being chosen one of "the golden dozen" would result in a bonus running into the millions. Even a twenty-seven-year old associate at a corporate law firm gets a $30,000 Christmas bonus.

I can recall a host of students over the years including many at NYU in the last two decades who told me "you have changed my life" or that my course was the best they had ever taken. And my honor amounts to a piece of paper and $1,000 (before 38 percent income taxes)? I tell my best students and have been doing so for a decade to go to law school. At least in the legal profession there is a rational reward system.

My distress over my teaching at NYU was especially hardened by the refusal of the History Department to let me teach a course on medieval and modern Jewish history even though my book on the subject, *The Sacred Chain*, was a selection of the Jewish Book Club in this country and a near best-seller in Britain, where it was favorably reviewed in a dozen newspapers and was the subject of two BBC radio interviews and one on SKY TV with me.

It seems my book on the Jews offers too secular a view of Jewish history to satisfy the rabbis in the NYU Judaic studies department, and they persuaded four successive history chairs not to let me go into competition with their Orthodox interpretation. One history chair, one of those leftist women hired when I was dean, suggested I teach the course but under a false title. "How about the history of Bosnia?" I suggested. She did not respond, being too busy fighting for workers' and women's rights to worry about mine.

By 1987 I was at loose ends and I accepted the invitation of two Israeli friends in the Tel Aviv University History Department to come there for a year as Fulbright Professor. So in April 1988, still only fifty-eight years old, I sat in my apartment in Netanya watching the sun come up out of the Mediterranean and contemplated once again what I should do with the rest of my life.

Writing history books for the widest possible audience seemed the only alternative I had left.

❖ 6 ❖

WRITING
AND TEACHING

I have had three careers. The first was that of a conventional academic engaged in teaching and scholarly writing. The second was that of university administrator. The third, which began in 1981 after I was summarily and unjustly fired as Dean of the Faculty of Arts and Science at NYU, has been that of professional writer.

It turned out that meant writer of history books, predominantly of the Middle Ages, not as a matter of choice but of necessity. I did not succeed at other kinds of writing, and at the end of the day it was my books about the Middle Ages that mostly gained a commercial market.

In 2002 I am a former academic and failed university administrator who has published some eighteen books, eleven of them about the Middle Ages in Western Europe. There are somewhere close to a million copies of my medieval books in print.

The Civilization of the Middle Ages (1994) is in its twenty-first paperback printing. *Inventing the Middle Ages* (1991) was a National Book

Critics Circle finalist for criticism and received a citation from NBCC for "literary excellence." It is now in its fifteenth paperback printing. The director of the Center for Medieval Studies at the University of York in Britain, Mark Ormrod, said in a review that *Inventing* was "worth its weight in gold." *In the Wake of the Plague*, a book about the Black Death of 1348–50 and its social impact (2001), went through four hardcover printings with sales of somewhere around forty thousand copies world-wide. This book achieved my heart's desire; it was on the *New York Times* best-seller list for three weeks. The paperback edition, published by HarperCollins in April 2002, has also had a print run of forty thousand copies. A Japanese translation is under way.

Medieval Lives (1994) is in its eleventh paperback printing but has underperformed in the market. A Japanese translation exists and a Korean translation may also have occurred. *The Sacred Chain*, my secular version of Jewish history, is about 25 percent devoted to the Middle Ages. This book (1995) is in its fifth paperback printing and was a commercial failure although it has become something of a cult book among secularized Jews.

My best book from an academic point of view, *Imagining the Law* (1997), a history of English common law and three quarters devoted to the Middle Ages was a resounding commercial failure; it is out of print except, peculiarly, for India.

My most ambitious effort at a non-medieval book, *The American Century* (1996), a history of twentieth-century culture in the United States and Western Europe, had small market penetration, although it was chosen by the New York Public Library as one of the twenty-five most memorable books of the year. On this book I had a collaborator, Mindy Cantor, who dealt with the visual arts and also made important suggestions on intellectual history. I had several collaborators for *The*

Encyclopedia of the Middle Ages, particularly its editor Harold Rabinowitz. I wrote the introduction and some twenty of the longer articles.

I am especially proud of *The Medieval Reader* (1994) which is now in its tenth printing because this book, an anthology of medieval writings, is organized topically rather than chronologically and provides within its three hundred pages a deep immersion into the medieval social and thought world.

What have I learned from this turmoil of publication addressed primarily to the general reader ("the trade") and secondarily the college student? First, there is a big market for books about the Middle Ages. Secondly, at all publishing houses there are well-educated, insightful, and idealistic editors. Hugh Van Dusen at HarperCollins and Bruce Nichols at Simon and Schuster have been especially helpful to me.

Third, literary agents are of great value not only in negotiating contracts and monitoring royalties but also as critical readers of manuscript drafts. I have done a dozen books with Alexander Hoyt. He is a scholar and a gentleman as well as a good business manager. He has profoundly shaped my life in my third career. Fourth, at all publishing houses the promotion and advertising staff is underfunded and short of qualified personnel.

Fifth, whether a book finds a substantial market or not is unpredictable. Writing for the trade is a roll of the dice.

Sixth, the bookstore chains have been my friends, especially Barnes and Noble where close to half my sales have occurred. I have not done well sales-wise in the private bookstores with a couple of exceptions in Washington, D.C. and Portland, Oregon (respectively Politics and Prose and Powell's).

My method of work is highly idiosyncratic. I take almost no notes but store all information gained from reading in my brain. I have never used a computer. Like many writers of my generation I am bound to the typewriter—up to 1999, a 1968 model Smith Corona; since then, a 1978 IBM Selectric III.

A book takes me usually two to three years with the last year being devoted to writing anywhere between three and six drafts. The best writing, for me, comes not when I am confident, relaxed, happy, and self-satisfied but rather when I have sustained an unpleasant shock—a car accident, a troublesome letter from the IRS about a tax return, trouble with my landlord, a domestic crisis, or insults and abuse from a group of academic colleagues. Then I write to affirm my own dignity, humanity, and autonomy that is seriously threatened by bad happenings and dangerous persons.

I have a bipolar personality (manic-depressive). And my best writing also comes in my manic phase, as any psychiatrist could predict. But I have to keep working through my depressed state because the manic phase endures only 20 percent of the time. Fifty milligrams of Prozac every day since 1996 has helped my productivity, and I have also greatly benefited from the ministrations of two first-class women therapists, successively Lynda Zweben-Howland and Gail C. Eisenberg MD. I have no transference with male psychotherapists.

I start on a book with six months to a year of omnivorous nonstop reading. Somewhere after a year, the book jells into a chapter outline which will only modestly ever be departed from. When I am at the height of productivity, whole sentences, even paragraphs will appear in my mind, usually as I fall asleep or have just awaken. Sometimes a word or short phrase will trigger a whole chapter.

I do not think of my audience as being other than mature adults, highly intelligent, and reasonably well read. I do not have academics in mind when I write, and except for an anthology or encyclopedia, I do not envisage student reactions. In a late draft, student needs will be recognized.

I have done the routine promotion activities: dozens of TV and radio interviews, public lectures (as many as five hundred fee-paying people at the Smithsonian on June 27, 2001) and bookstore talks and signings. I have no idea how these activities sell copies of my books. They stroke my ego, I am sure, and inspire me to go on writing.

I can only write on a well-fed stomach, fostering obesity. I do not drink while I write and drink very little otherwise. I smoked a pipe heavily until 1983 and none since. I quit smoking cold turkey. I am frequently inspired to write by reading beautiful history on just about any topic and well outside the Middle Ages. Except for newspapers and magazines, all my leisure is history. It doesn't matter much whether one writes from a traditional humanist or postmodernist point of view. What matters is making the subject matter come alive for the reader.

I can only write four to five pages a day. Sometimes I write a page or two as poetry and print it out as prose. There is no pleasure in life greater than receiving a substantial royalty check. It is better than sex. I always write while baroque music is playing on the radio or phonograph.

For more than a decade the now leading neo-conservative intellectual journal in the United States has been *The New Criterion*, an expensively printed monthly, lavishly funded by the John M. Olin Foundation, the wealthiest rightist foundation in the United States (as the Ford Foundation is the wealthiest leftist foundation). *The New Criterion* is skillfully edited by Hilton Kramer, sometime chief art critic for the *New York Times*, and his protégé, Roger Kimball, who also writes books about the leftist penetration into and intellectual corruption of the American university by "tenured radicals" since the 1960s.

Well-known rightists from inside the academy such as Boston University's John Silber and CUNY's Gertrude Himmelfarb contribute articles on this theme, which amount to a nostalgic yearning for the old humanistic, Anglophilic, center-right culture. I have yearnings along that line myself and especially when Kramer himself articulates his journal's conservative doctrine. I respond in a positive manner viscerally if not cognitively to what he says.

But there is a crossroad where I and the neo-cons part company, and they have no use for my books and fail to review them, even negatively. I am a relativist or social constructivist. And beyond that to some extent, I am a psychological determinist when it comes to critique of academic and cultural discourses. I believe that inevitably all ideas, on campus and off, are substantially—although not entirely—shaped by changes in the structure of the societal ambiance.

Further, I believe that there are instances when ideas and scholarly work are recognizably affected by the psychological development of an individual thinker and writer or artist. This is a Freudian position. These two relativist approaches—as idea, book, or art form takes shape relative to sociology and psychology—have had an impact on all my historical and biographical writing. This has made me anathema to the neo-cons.

In 1991 after a year long evaluation process by a blue ribbon faculty search committee for a new Dean of Arts and Science at Boston University, the committee chaired by a former medical school dean and dominated by the presence of the English humanist and literary critic Christopher Ricks put forth my name to then President John Silber as their only nominee. Silber refused to appoint me and canceled the search. When I write to Kramer and Kimball commenting on something they have said in *The New Criterion* (usually that it is a mistake to think that postmodernist doctrine is only a leftist phenomenon; it can also be compatible with rightist ideas), they ignore me. Gertrude Himmelfarb has for more than a decade publicly made clear her contempt for me.

So here I am, a divided psyche, sympathetic to neo-conservatives, longing for a reaffirmation of the old Anglophilic humanist culture I grew up in but also driven by my understanding of human experience to espouse relativist ideas that are anathema to the intellectual right. They think there is only one truth and they have the power to gain it by their reason and adherence to tradition. They think sociology, anthropology, and psychology have nothing to do with constructing a culture. I find this untenable and contrary to human experience.

I worship, along with other academics who can loosely be called postmodernists, at the shrine of Claude Lévi-Strauss, Michel Foucault, and Jacques Derrida. I tried in my book *The American Century: Varieties of Culture in Modern Times* to articulate their thoughts and explain their importance.

Lévi-Strauss' *Tristes tropiques* (1955; *A World on the Wane*) is after Freud's *Die Traumdeutung* (1900; *The Interpretation of Dreams*) the most important book of the twentieth century. Lévi-Strauss claims that we live in unified systemic mental and material structures that determine the individual's identity and behavior.

Foucault identifies all institutions and movements, even allegedly humanitarian ones like the insane asylum, the penitentiary, or feminism, as instruments of class and group power. This view is in the Marxist tradition, spiced with Friedrich Nietzsche's extreme relativism and resentment of elites.

Derrida views all texts as inherently unstable and self-contradictory, given to fragmentation (deconstruction) and revealing counter-texts underneath. This is Freud applied to written word culture.

These ideas seem rational and convincing to me. I am not much disturbed when they become vehicles for provocative behavior by academics, such as offering courses on pornography, or cutting back in the teaching of Western Civilization, or replacing texts with films, or teaching the history of jazz and rock alongside diplomacy and economics. The proponents of the new academic culture who worship at the shrine of the three French theorists as well as of Marx, Freud, and Nietzsche, can and do sometimes act foolishly and distastefully, but that is of no long-term importance.

All cultures have extreme acolytes, including those of the old academic culture of the 1950s that the neo-cons now glorify and reify so intensely. The extreme acolytes of the old culture were not provocative. They were just boring.

I subscribe for a few dollars a year to the publications of *Accuracy in Academia*, a right-wing organization operating out of Washington. Here is their lead complaint for June, 1999: "They're deluging students with bizarre left-wing courses—Swarthmore's *Lesbian Novels since World War II*, Colorado's *The Social Construction of Reality*, and UC-Santa Barbara's *Black Marxism* are a few examples." That these courses are left-wing I have no doubt. But I can see nothing bizarre about them. They are appropriate subjects for inquiry at the college level.

Are Plato, Dante, Shakespeare, and Kant more appropriate subjects at the college level and more central to college education? *Yes, and ideally students should have mastered the classics before going on to avant-garde and specialized subjects.* The problem is that no one has figured out how to provide for the immersion of large numbers of students in the former so that a cognitive process occurs before pursuing the latter.

Furthermore, teaching the classics is a very challenging task that requires extraordinary capability of intellect and communication. The academic profession does not pay well enough to attract a sufficient number of extraordinary teachers. Nearly all superior people have in recent decades eschewed Ph.D. programs in the humanities and have gone to elite law schools which are the avenues to infinitely greater material rewards and social status than academia provides.

Just because a course on one of the classics of Western Civilization is offered does not mean it will be more productive and enjoyable for the student than the courses on lesbian novels and Marxism. As a medievalist of some stature on the NYU campus I was invited a few years ago to give a guest lecture in a course devoted entirely to the text of Dante's *Divine Comedy*. I spoke near the end of the semester when the students should have been brimming with their mastery of the text and holding sophisticated opinions on Dante's complex thought-world. I found nothing like this however. The students had learned very little about Dante that semester.

Frequently, even normally a classic text is taught this way: the professor reads a half dozen lines and explicates them at length. Students take notes and regurgitate the professor's explications by rote on the final exams. I am not sure that this is better than a well-taught course on lesbianism or Marxism, where intellectual engagement might actually occur.

In the history of American higher education there has been a cycle on the one hand of stressing a core curriculum of what a culturally literate person must know, and on the other the free elective system, first introduced at Harvard around 1895 by Charles W. Eliot and today still in place, not at Harvard but at nearby Brown University.

The free elective system is predicated on the assumption that students individually know what they want to learn and indeed they cannot be kept from learning it somehow, in or out of class. So it is best to let them choose all their own courses. If that means ten courses on lesbian literature or Marxism, so be it. They will have thereby learned something substantial and can move on from there if they are motivated. Foisting pabulum of core classics on them will only bore and frustrate them and they will retain nothing at all that is meaningful to them, so say the advocates of the free elective system. I have never been able to choose firmly between these two theories of liberal education.

What have I learned about trade publishers? All the conditioned responses, the inevitable fuss, the swallowing of distinguished imprints by conglomerates affects me hardly at all *unless* "the suits," the managers from the conglomerates and their representatives as heads of publishing houses (often women), impinge on the freedom and judgment and good taste of editors at the companies. This happens more than it should as the conglomerates look for a 15 percent annual profit margin from the trade houses they have bought up whereas trade publishing has always been a small 3 percent to 6 percent annual profit margin enterprise.

When the suits become impatient for profits and naively demanding, the people they install at the heads of trade houses can turn into destructive and rash tyrants. A kind of reign of terror overcomes the publishing house. Good editors are either fired or driven into silence and extreme caution. Editors lose their capacity to exercise personal judgment and take risks with a new or previously unsuccessful author or a subject that seems remote from the TV-driven, middle-class culture. Thereby the integrity of public culture deteriorates.

Publishing houses today are organized into rigid vertical compartments: editorial, production, marketing, publicity, and promotion. Each entity operates according to its own code and to what it considers as its best institutional interests. Editors have often some influence with the production people but not enough to prevent ghastly errors in published books.

Whole lines mysteriously disappear from the published text that were still there in proof. Captions are left off pictures. To add insult to injury, reviewers, especially in the more popular media, either out of naiveté or the meanest malevolence are prone to blame authors for mistakes in production of the book. When computerized typesetting came along a decade or so ago, authors were assured the glaring print errors were a thing of the past. If anything they have become more prevalent and severe—a whole line of the text excised instead of just a typo in one word.

Yet editors usually have some influence on the production staff. The impact disappears with regard to those autonomous entities, the marketing and promotion and publicity departments. They will make their own decision on how to market and whether and how to publicize a book. They love to shoot fish in a barrel: marketing and promoting a new book by an already highly visible, best-selling author or media personality that is likely to do well in any case. The marketers and publicists loathe the thought of promoting a book by a relatively unknown author about what seems (to their notoriously uninformed minds) an obscure subject remote from the interests of the lay reader, like the Amazon, Borders, and Barnes and Noble browser.

In other words, when marketing and promoting a book requires hard work, ingenuity, and good information, they abstain. Editors of long standing in the company can seemingly do nothing about this default because in cases of dispute, the suits or their representatives in the executive offices will always take the side of the marketers and publicists. They all want to sell and promote a book by Erica Jong, which requires no promotion, not one by Erica's obscure sometime teacher at Columbia, Norman Cantor.

Even when a publicist condescends to arrange a book tour for a mid-list writer, the results are liable to be very painful. The author can find himself speaking in a bookstore on a university campus to three people in the audience. Abominable travel and hotel arrangements for the author in distant cities and abuse by the media are the outcome.

Thus it was that I found myself in a Cleveland suburb on a gray, snowy February day before being interviewed at a TV station on tape for later broadcast. The interview for once went well, which means the interviewer or her producer had actually read some of the book and asked intelligent questions. The interview ran for more than an hour and I was told it would be edited down to a 50-minute broadcast the coming weekend. I was delighted. As I was sitting on my coat, I asked, "By the way, is your TV station affiliated with a network?"

"Didn't anyone tell you? We are part of the Home Shopping Network."

My disgust was tempered by an epiphanic vision of five thousand copies of my book an hour being sold over the air. When I imparted this vision to my interviewer, she said, "Oh no! Your book would never sell well enough to make it suitable for on the air sales. The FCC requires us to do an hour of educational programming per week and you are it for this week."

"Oh," I said, "I understand," not hiding my humiliation. "When will this tape actually be broadcast?"

"At 5:00 A.M. Sunday."

There was the time I taxied across Boston in a snowstorm to the offices of the *Boston Globe* to be interviewed by the religion editor there about my book, only to be told by the editor that although he had a copy from the publisher for five weeks, he had somehow never gotten around to reading any of it. There were times when a truth panel of Orthodox Jews, dressed in black suits and black hats, and with long beards and curly sidelocks, who disliked my secular view of Jewish history, followed me from a bookstore presentation to another in Manhattan in order to denounce me as a *mishumid* (a Christian convert) and *apicurus* (epicurean lying secularist).

There were a few good moments on the publicist arranged book tour—especially an hour interview on radio to five million people by G. Gordon Liddy of Watergate infamy about my book on the old common law, which prompted four convicts in a Louisiana prison to write me begging that I should handle their umpteenth appeal—the beginning of a John Grisham novel.

Becoming a professional writer of trade books and publishing a book every two years, or even sooner, gives entry to a whole new way of passing time—playing the bookstore game. As the day of publication approaches, so does the author's anxiety rise as to the fate of one's new book in the bookstores, especially in the chains like Barnes and Noble and Borders. Will the book be available in the bookstore? Will it be found in a pile of half dozen copies on a table devoted to new publications near the front door of the store? Or will it be found in one or two copies in the history section at the back of the store next to the washrooms?

I confess that until I became a professional writer, I rarely entered a bookstore. If I wanted a book, I simply phoned the customer service line of its publisher and ordered it on a credit card, the book arriving by UPS three days later.

It took me awhile, however, to realize that with respect to the chains, how many copies they order and where they place them are normally predetermined by arrangement between the marketing division of the publisher and the buyer for the chains, the publisher making certain concessions to get an intense and highly visible placement. It is therefore more the publisher's faith in a book's trade potential than the bookstore's that determines the book's fate. I learned to save myself those agonizing visits to Barnes and Noble or Borders and simply have my literary agent find out the publisher's marketing plan—usually disappointing—for the book.

The private, independent bookstores still provide opportunities for the chase, for the bookstore game. The independent (non-chain) bookstores are unpredictable as to how they treat my books. They may order ten copies; they may order none. Just flip a coin. It's a crapshoot.

Sometimes I wonder how I came to take on the three worst careers —except for mining in Siberia, the needle trades in Indonesia, and cleaning the washrooms of bus stations—namely academia, university administration, and writing for the trade. But at other times I think I have been blessed by two of these three careers—teaching undergraduates and writing for the public.

Not administration: Don Riddle was right; I was the Ted Williams of university administrators; I could hit .400 but I was not a team player; for all his prowess Ted Williams never led the Red Sox to a world championship.

I think the biggest drawback to university administration is the physical and psychological strain of constantly meeting with mischievous or incompetent managerial colleagues and frequently facing faculty and students unhappy about something—and usually having grounds for their complaints, which it was difficult or well-nigh impossible to resolve.

The successful university administrators today are the cool ones, like Corbally of Illinois or Oliva of NYU. They stand above the fray, have no firm opinions about anything except to erect more and bigger buildings and fashion better athletic teams. Certainly they do not become involved in the ideological conflicts and culture wars among the faculty.

The only prominent hot-button university administrator I know of was John Silber, first dean at Texas-Austin (where, of course, he got fired) and then the long-serving and immensely controversial president of Boston University. He came on like a blowtorch both publicly and privately in expressing opinions and shaping his policies and decisions around these strong opinions. He was not reluctant, indeed he was eager to stay with the old culture and condemn the new culture and leftist positions. He actually hired and fired several faculty and deans based on their political beliefs: neo-cons in, lefties out.

Silber is the case model held up to show that hot, high-contact university administrators can be successful. But Silber had a Board of Trustees at Boston University whom he had mesmerized into slavish devotion to himself. In that he was fortunate. His vice president and deans were mere staff sergeants in the ranks. He used secretaries and administrative assistants to help in his campaigns for public office. He invested a substantial part of the university's endowment in a risky and unsuccessful startup biotech company—and convinced some older faculty to lose their life savings in this bizarre venture. Once Silber had decided to make a huge fiscal commitment to an academic program—in his case the Physics Department—nothing could convince him that he had made a mistake and ought to retrench.

Successful indeed Silber was as president of BU following the hot-button, hyperactive ideological approach. But a cooler, more moderate, and austere president would have been even more successful there. By 1970 a lot of young people from all over the country wanted to go to college in Boston. Harvard had no room; Boston College was too Catholic; Brandeis too Jewish; Northeastern too proletarian. All BU had to do was open its doors, put up decent classroom and lab buildings, and hire a smattering of first rate faculty. It was a no-lose situation.

As a university president, I would have been closer to the Silber than the Corbally/Oliva model. I might have been a terrific success but possibly also a dreadful failure.

There is no drawback to teaching except the ingratitude of students. They tell me I have changed their lives, that mine is the best college course they have ever taken, etc. But they almost never think that maybe I would like a present reflecting their gratitude. I am just old Norm the professor slinking off to die on my inadequate pension.

Former students of mine will notice my tiny obituary (if that) in the *Times* and say to their spouses over breakfast in their lavish condos: I knew that guy; he was a great teacher; please pass the marmalade.

Each year I told the pre-law students in my common law course that ten years hence when they are speeding downtown in their BMWs on the way to their Wall Street corporate law offices and notice a seedy old man standing with a beggar's styrofoam cup on the street, that will be me; stop and throw in a dollar. I will need it. This image always evokes a few laughs and total disbelief. I am serious.

Only four times in forty-five years of teaching have students shown material appreciation. When I left Columbia in 1966 they presented me with an antique map of England. In 1974 my best student at Binghamton, Charles Dellheim, at the time of his graduation gave me a bottle of exceptional vintage French wine. At my sixty-second birthday with the help of my wife there was a surprise party. And best of all, after I had expounded in a medieval history course at NYU in 1986 on Sancerre as the white wine of French medieval kings and Chateauneuf du Pape as the wine of the fourteenth-century Avignon popes, two students promptly went to the nearest liquor store and presented me with a bottle of each expensive vintage.

I have had four exceptional undergraduate students in my forty-two years of teaching. My best student at Binghamton, Charles Dellheim, is now the chairman of the History Department at Boston University. Kate Ludwig Jansen was awarded the Prix de Rome and the annual prize of the American Catholic Historical Association for her Princeton dissertation on thirteenth-century Italian spirituality. Michael Stein after Harvard Law School got a Ph.D. in legal history at Cambridge and now teaches at the College of William and Mary Law School. The most remarkable undergraduate I have ever taught was the artist Frank Stella at Princeton in the 1950s. He wrote his senior thesis under my supervision and he could have been a very important art historian.

I had a graduate student once at Columbia, a scrawny priest from Staten Island, Bernard McGinn, who is now at the University of Chicago—one of the three or four leading American medieval historians of his generation. And I recently had a doctoral student, Judith Potter, who is the finest researcher among any students I have ever had. She is doing a book on merchant families in fifteenth-century northern Germany that will remind academics of Fernand Braudel's seminal 1952 book on the Mediterranean economy.

It is true that teaching has great non-material satisfactions. No matter how depressed I am, put me in front of a class and I am likely to become animated emotionally as well as intellectually activated. Teaching is a kind of love which St. Augustine defined as a union of wills. But the physical side to love is not entirely absent from teaching. Hardly a year has passed since 1960 when I have taught women students that I have not had erotic feelings toward one of my women students. The feminists say this is bad, of course. But I have never so much as held the hand of my Beatrices, let alone had an affair with them. It is not for lack of erotic feelings; it is for lack of courage.

I do not believe that students today, taken as a group are inferior in quality to what they were in 1960. They are not normally as text-oriented, but they are orally and visually more acute and they write better because much writing had been demanded of them in high school and their first year of college.

All the students want now, like four decades ago, is a well-structured course curriculum and clear and forceful lectures with occasional discussions, that I prefer to do one-on-one in my office rather than by taking up classroom time. The proportion of students from my last common law course taught at NYU in the spring of 1999 who will go on to successful careers in law was not less than the class I taught in the same subject at Columbia in the spring of 1961.

I passionately believe that, give me a small class of twenty students in any subject in the humanities—literature, philosophy, history—and irrespective of their race, class, or gender, I can get them to learn and perform well, and at least half of the class will deservedly get "A's" and write very good papers and exams.

I once, in the early seventies, had a chance to test this belief when Brooklyn College was forced into open admissions. A wily associate dean there who favored open admissions got me to drive down from Binghamton one day a week and for six hours teach medieval history to a class of so-called remedial students. All but two of the twenty students were people of color. I did not pander to them. I used the same curriculum and reading list at the highly selective Harpur College at Binghamton. I had eighteen-year-olds from disadvantaged backgrounds reading *The Song of Roland,* Augustine's *Confessions,* and *The Little Flowers of Saint Francis.* I taught under the most favorable of circumstances—not only a small class size but with support from a very capable teaching assistant.

Together we worked a full six hours weekly with the students. They wrote a three-page paper every week, which was carefully reviewed with them. I lectured for two hours. We had ninety minutes of discussion. I never had a better class. The grades were terrific and honestly assigned.

The problem in college education is not with the students; it is with the faculty. Ever since Harvard's James Conant in 1946 legislated research as the sole criterion for tenure, the higher education establishment has failed its consumers.

But only momentarily do I think about that. I am no longer out to reform higher education, but rather to live within it and enjoy myself. The teacher should no more worry about the shape of higher education than a first-rate painter brood about what nonsense this week is going on at Sotheby's or the Chelsea galleries. Van Gogh did not sell one picture in his lifetime. So be it.

A college teacher on the first day of class is like a painter facing a fresh, empty canvas. How shall I fill up this space? What themes shall I expound? How shall I lay the color on the canvas? How shall I make love collectively to 60 or 150 students? This is what the teacher has in mind. And no one can take it away from the artist-teacher. She or he will make her or his own decisions about what happens in each class.

This is one of the few truly liberating experiences in the world. That is why I hate team teaching and why only very severe illness—or my wife's giving birth—has ever led me to cancel a class. I once got chickenpox from my young son and turned up to teach at Columbia. Dick Morris said: "Go home. Maybe it's smallpox. How am I going to explain to the dean when the whole class is wiped out?"

At Princeton as a graduate student I took a course on teaching a freshman Western Civilization lecture from Gordon Craig, later chairman at Stanford and author of many good books on German history. I couldn't understand how he got the timing down so perfectly, how his lecture ended climactically just as the clock struck the hour. Easy, it turned out. In the last ten minutes of the lecture have flexible material you can leave in or take out as time allows—quotations from a document, amusing anecdotes, etc.

We gave our trial lectures and then Craig perfectly mimicked each of us, letting us know how badly we looked and sounded. Craig's famous lecture on Hitler ended with five minutes of hysterical babbling in German, better than Charlie Chaplin in *The Great Dictator*. This is the kind of highly articulated teaching I did in my early years. Midway through my career I just let it come from my heart. Either way it worked.

Trade writing for the general public is also a form of personal liberation. Academic writing of monographs and articles is not. In academic writing the real thrust is in the footnotes. I have successfully challenged graduate students to show me the footnotes for an article or chapter with the text covered up and I will immediately construct the argument above.

Textbook writing is very burdensome because you have to write about subjects you don't believe in as actually having happened, like the Thirty Years War. As elite colleges have snootily abandoned textbooks for miscellaneous readings, the textbook in the humanities is largely confined to community colleges and low-end state colleges whose students, the education experts say, read at grade nine level. So textbook writing today takes away half your vocabulary. It is like making sausages with discarded pieces of meat. In trade writing it is just me and the blank paper—I prefer ivory.

Sometimes when I write I may feel my agent or editor looking over my shoulder and grimacing, this won't sell. Instantly I can conjure the pale scowling visages of the Ivy League medievalist establishment saying stop, not again with your vulgarity. But it does not take much effort to shake off these impediments.

Writing provides a sense of freedom and mastery that is otherwise rarely gained in life. The polarized dialectics of the war between the old and new academic cultures dissipate, and I draw from both sides what I need to communicate my sense of human experience and cultural structures. The vast repertoire of historical learning of the past century becomes malleable and applicable to any idea, theme, sentence, or word.

I know that completing a book will lead to the agonies and disappointments deriving from the incompetence and negligence of publishers and that down the track lurk my old academic enemies waiting to assault and dehumanize me again in bad reviews.

But for the moment I am happy and free to create my own world, my own figurement of the past. And out there among the educated public there are thousands of people waiting to read my books. I have become a minor brand name in the book trade. In spite of publishers' usual failure to distribute, market, and promote my books effectively and in spite of crabbed old men and jealous young academics trying to prevent me from communicating to the public, I can go on my way of writing.

As for the culture wars, so politicized and polarized, and shaped by the machinations of iconic power brokers, I am free to take what I want from both the old culture I grew up in and went to school in and the new culture I came to appreciate after 1960. I carry water neither for the right nor the left.

I have run into trouble in my teaching and writing about Jewish history. There are two themes in my history of the Jews, *The Sacred Chain* (1994), that are anathema to the suburban rabbis and the Orthodox Jewish community in general—as well as to many Conservative and nominally Reform Jews. First, I said that Jewish history as presented in the Bible for the period before the tenth century B.C.E. is mythical—brilliant fiction concocted between 600 and 300 B.C.E., some of it written in Iraq, some in Jerusalem. The purpose was to give the Hebrews a sense of identity and destiny and a historic claim to the land of Zion. Abraham, Moses, and the whole story of the Exodus cannot be verified after more than a century of archaeological work in Egypt, the Sinai, and Israel and have to be regarded as mythic fiction. This secular view—by no means held only by me—undermines the legitimacy of the *halacha* (Jewish religious law) as well as Zionist claims to a historical and moral right to the land of Israel over the Palestinians.

Secondly, what is found offensive in my book is my view of Jewish domestic history from the sixth to the end of the nineteenth century as shaped by a narrow often-intermarried elite of rabbis and capitalists, from which the great emigration to America after 1880 finally liberated the Jewish masses. There is also nothing very new in this view; nearly all rabbis hate to see it propounded by an ethnically Jewish historian with reputable credentials.

My first teaching job in Winnipeg in 1950–51 was instructing on Jewish history in an Orthodox high school for students headed for rabbinical training in the United States. One of these students became a professor of Talmud at the Jewish Theological Seminary in New York. Another became a thriving rock concert promoter in Chicago and Los Angeles. After I got the job in Winnipeg, I visited one of those elite learned Jewish capitalists, a big man in the fur auction business. He had a splendid private library on Jewish history, all the important books written in English and Yiddish, and he gave me full access to this library.

Of course in those days there could be no thought of taking a Ph.D. in Jewish history—unless I was prepared to teach in a horrible rabbinical seminary. At Princeton and Oxford I hid my deep knowledge of Jewish history. I came out of the intellectual closet only at Columbia where one of the two or three leading Jewish historians in the world, Salo Baron, had an office three doors from mine. At least twice a month for four years until Baron retired, I visited him in his office, drank strong tea, and talked about fine points of Jewish history. Because the chair of the Columbia History Department, Richard Morris, was the son of a Brooklyn rabbi, I thought it was safe to blow my cover.

My father was "*Kol Yisroel*," one of the poor Jews from Eastern Europe. He knew how the rabbis and their capitalist allies had exploited and abused the Jewish masses through the centuries. I inherited his resentment and his secular attitudes, although he did attend synagogue on the High Holidays. So did I, reading an English novel hidden behind the boring medieval prayer book.

My wife is committed to Jewish religious and cultural traditions. She serves on the Board of a Reform synagogue in Sag Harbor, Long Island. I have no taste for this. In my later years Mindy has become more committed to Jewish religious traditions, including the Kabbalah and other mystical texts. She closely studies the Hebrew Bible and the Talmud, and she attends seminars on Jewish lore. Meanwhile I have become more secular and less sympathetic to Jewish traditions.

Since December 1999 I have lived in South Florida where my daughter resides. It is in Florida that I now do my writing, with only occasional trips north to use the Princeton and NYU libraries.

I have absented myself from my house in Sag Harbor in the Hamptons. In a small room on the second floor of this Dutch Colonial house, built as a workingman's cottage in 1910, but renovated and expanded since then, I wrote eight books in the nineties. It was, however, the one book I wrote in my Florida apartment, directly facing the South Atlantic, that became a *New York Times* national best-seller.

I think back through all the blows, slurs, insults, and prejudicial acts I suffered because I was born a Jew, from being beaten up by Ukrainian gangs when I was a child in Manitoba to my mentor Ted Mommsen telling me in 1953: "You have to be much better than the Gentiles if you want an academic appointment."

I followed Ted Mommsen's injunction. I was better than the Gentiles, also known as the Medieval Academy of America, the disciplinary association, and the Ivy League History Departments. No one else among professional medievalists has succeeded in communicating the result of current scholarship and research to a very wide audience.

The Medieval Academy Fellows address each other. I address the educated world at large. Their books sell in the hundreds, mine in the thousands. In the capability of directly communicating with the trade market, of seeing one of my books on the *New York Times* best-seller list, of watching annually the number of printings of a half dozen books steadily rise—this experience is deeply satisfying and not only because of the material rewards.

The bringing of the academic's Middle Ages to the inner circle of contemporary culture, this is my achievement and no one else in the Anglophone world has come close to matching my record as a professional writer of non-fiction books about the Middle Ages.

The cultural war between traditional humanism and radical post-modernism, played out at the extremes as a struggle between objectivity and subjectivity, this polarity that reached its peak in the 1990s, is now coming to be superseded by another spectrum of choices.

Is historical writing to be addressed to a small group of academics or is it to be communicated to the educated world at large? I stand with the latter proposition, that history books are communicable to and accessible by the educated public at large. The ultimate task and obligation of a historian is to bring this kind of illumination to as wide an audience as possible.

Take the learning about the past still being added to daily by academic research and enclose and mold it within a literature that stirs the imagination. This is the program I am following in my third career.

Whether a medieval historian is addressing at most a few dozen other scholars world-wide, or whether she is addressing thousands of readers among the public at large—this is one great issue in medieval studies today.

Another related but still distinct issue is whether medieval people should be regarded as having a same or similar mindset to ourselves or whether they should be seen as operating within a very different intellectual framework.

As an example: Are the eating disorders of medieval nuns to be seen as part of the development of spirituality or should these practitioners of "holy feast and holy fast" be regarded as people with severe neuroses? My view is that medieval people operated within a set of values and concepts that are the same or very similar to those of today. A nun suffering from a severe eating disorder today may be garnering some spiritual points at the margin, but essentially hers is a psychological problem not a religious quest.

The great writers and thinkers of medieval Europe were functioning within the same framework of ideas as those we utilize today. I am of the opinion that our concepts of human behavior are the same as those of medieval people once you get beyond a thin veneer of language differences. Freudian concepts are, therefore, applicable to medieval consciousness and sub-consciousness. Medieval ideas of love, of power, of gender, and of class divisions are also within our frame of reference.

This is the second great issue in medieval studies today. Here again as in the question to whom are we speaking about the Middle Ages, I am in the minority.

But the second issue affects resolution of the first. If my writings about the Middle Ages receive the attention of many thousands (not so much students as mature adult readers impulse buying at Barnes and Noble), then I have a chance to make an impression even though the feminist-dominated academic medievalists currently want the medieval mindset to be seen as fundamentally different from our own.

In the Ivy League and the Medieval Academy of America frustration reigns that my universalist point of view—that the writers of the twelfth and thirteenth centuries are also within our frame of reference—is making an impact on the educated public. Academia is a series of little totalitarian entities—the word goes forth from Harvard, Columbia, and Princeton of the line to be followed and the doctoral students do so, being too anxious about their career possibilities to dissent. But no longer a dependent academic, I can say what I believe.

Anyone who sets out to write about the Middle Ages has encountered two sets of polarities about which the author must make a judgment. The first spectrum involves the polarities of addressing a small group of scholars and graduate students—at most five hundred people world-wide—versus writing for a very broad audience of literate adults, numbering in the hundreds of thousands, if you, as a writer with adequate promotion and marketing support from your publisher, can attract them to purchase your book, particularly in a cheap paperback edition after two or three hardcover printings.

Ninety-eight percent of academic writers on the Middle Ages never face up to this polarity. They just write for the scholars. Writing for the general audience is difficult because detailed contexts have to be explained to readers who never took a medieval history course in college and high school or have forgotten what they learned in these courses. But the detailed context has to be subtly introduced or it will bore the readers or appear to be grossly pandering to them. The most successful writer of a nonfiction medieval history book for the general reader was Barbara W. Tuchman. The runners-up were Emmanuel Le Roy Ladurie, Michael Clanchy, and myself.

The second spectrum on which the medievalist writer must make a choice involves the polarity of what is sometimes called historicism, the conviction that medieval people thought, wrote, and behaved differently from ourselves (e.g., eating disorders among nuns were grounded in expressions of spirituality) as against a universalist or sociological, psychological, and anthropological set of assumptions. Beyond differences in language and literary genres, medieval people thought, wrote, and behaved much as we do (e.g., nuns' eating disorders reflect psychiatric problems whether in the thirteenth century or today). Just as I belong to that 2 percent of academic medievalists who try to write for a general audience, I belong to a shrinking minority (perhaps 15 percent) of medieval historians who are universalists rather than historicists.

Any book I write about the Middle Ages will be governed by the needs of trade audiences and by universalist assumptions. These condition all my books.

What shape the book takes follows along one of two lines—the book is either longitudinal, that is long-term narrative or it is microcosmic. In the latter case, it focuses closely on a particular event, person, or small group of people. You are either taking a filmic long shot with a wide angle lens or doing an intense closeup with a lens suitable for sharp focus detail. *The Civilization of the Middle Ages* was longitudinal in method and so was *Imagining the Law. Inventing the Middle Ages* and *In the Wake of the Plague* were microcosmic. *Inventing* focused as intimately as possible on twenty prominent medievalists of the twentieth century. *Plague* concentrated on a half dozen individuals and families deeply affected by the mortality in the Black Death of fourteenth-century England. Tuchman in *A Distant Mirror*, Ladurie in *Montaillou*, and Clanchy in *Abelard* showed their mastery of the microcosmic approach. Over time I have inclined to the microcosmic as against the longitudinal approach and I have gotten better at it.

The longitudinal approach to writing about the Middle Ages is understanding the medieval world from the outside in, moving from narrative objectivity to discovery of an inner secret behind the longitudinal projection. The microcosmic approach is understanding the Middle Ages from the inside out, building from sharp focus on individuals and particular events to a composite objective meaning.

In the first sixty-five years of the twentieth century the longitudinal projection dominated. Since then the microcosmic focus has been fashionable. If there is a single truth about the Middle Ages, it derives from a blending of the longitudinal and microcosmic projections.

The important point is to eschew methodological orthodoxy of one kind or another and recognize that the truth about the Middle Ages is a progressive and multi-faceted revelation communicated through a high degree of literary art.

As I look back in my seventy-second year at the trade books I have written, I notice how much darker and less idealistic my view of the Middle Ages has become. The book now called in its fourth edition, *The Civilization of the Middle Ages* is in its twentieth printing since 1994. It still retains 60 percent of the text of the first edition of 1963 and when I made major changes in the fourth edition of 1994, I consciously imitated the assumptions and style of the first edition. There are probably three hundred thousand copies of this book in print in one edition or another. It views the generative motif of the Middle Ages as applied idealism. Medieval history is the story of the effort made over twelve hundred years to realize, to put into institutional practice and social operations, certain dominating romantic ideas in the European and Mediterranean world.

Compare this attitude with that of my most recent book, *In the Wake of the Plague*, in which ideas are treated much more skeptically, even a bit cynically. The dominating forces for change in the medieval world are climatic, biomedical, and material. At the same time the book explores individuals as products of complex psychological and social forces, of private ambitions and family pressures. This world is much less idealistic than *The Civilization of the Middle Ages'* portrait.

This is a consequence of what happened to me in university administration from 1974 to 1981. My own motivations remained charged with moral idealism, but I found most others did not share this high-mindedness and used ideas as smoke screens to cover up cruelty, arrogance, and selfishness. As Tennyson's Ulysses said, "We are part of all that we have met."

That is why no set of historical assumptions is definitive. The happiness and sadness of our own lives shape the way we comprehend historical events and personalities.

❖ 7 ❖

KNOWING MORE
ABOUT ACADEME

I f this book has interested you in undertaking further scrutiny of academic life, I suggest the following.

Begin by seeing the 2001 film, *A Beautiful Mind*, directed by Ron Howard and starring Russell Crowe and Jennifer Connelly. It tells the story of the Princeton mathematician John Nash.

Academic novels are a genre of their own. The two best are written by British Academics: Charles P. Snow, *The Masters* (1951) and Malcolm Bradbury, *The History Man* (1974).

Academic autobiographies and biographies comprise another genre. The best memoirs are C. Vann Woodward, *Looking Back* (Baton Rouge: Louisiana State University Press, 1986) and Jane Tompkins, *A Life in School* (New York: Addison Wesley, 1996). Among biographies the best book, based on Harvard University Archives, is the biographical account of James B. Conant's Harvard presidency by Morton and Phyllis Keller (Cambridge, MA.: Harvard University Press, 2001). Additional books that provide insight into the structure and operation of universities are

Donald Kennedy, *Academic Duty* (Cambridge, MA.: Harvard University Press, 1997); John Guillory, *Cultural Capital: The Problem of Literary Canon Formation* (Chicago: University of Chicago Press, 1993); Bill Readings, *The University in Ruins* (Cambridge, MA.: Harvard University Press, 1996); Thomas Bender and Carl E. Schorske, eds., *American Academic Culture in Transformation* (Princeton: Princeton University Press, 1997); and André Schiffrin, ed., *The Cold War and the University* (New York: The New Press, 1997).

I have also learned much from close reading of two weeklies: the densely informative *Chronicle of Higher Education* and the funky and hilarious *London Times Higher Education Supplement.* An occasional article in *Change* magazine has been illuminating. I am a regular reader of *Daedalus* and *The American Scholar* but what I have learned from these two journals ostensibly devoted to American academic culture is very little. The *Princeton Alumni Weekly* and the *Daily Princetonian* have actually been more forthcoming with information and ideas.

For details on the development of medieval studies from 1895 to 1965, see Norman F. Cantor, *Inventing the Middle Ages* (New York: Morrow, 1991).

For an overview of intellectual and cultural history, 1910-present, that affected medieval studies, see Norman F. Cantor, *The American Century* (New York: Harper Collins, 1997).

INDEX